Mel Bay Presents

Songs of the Sea, Rivers, Lakes & Canals

Jerry Silverman

1. Songs, Popular
2. Folk-Songs
ISBN 1-56222-283-X
M14

ilverman

Cover illustration by Greg Ragland.

Contents

A Terrible Battle That
Happened of Late

The Yankee Man-Of-War

The "Yankee Man-Of-War" is the sloop *Ranger,* under the command of John Paul Jones, which cruised the Irish Sea in the spring of 1778, creating havoc along the British coast.

'Tis of a gal – lant Yan – kee ship that flew the stripes and stars; The whis – tl – ing wind from west – nor – west blew through her pitch – pine spars. With her star – board tacks a – board, my boys, she hung up to the gale. 'Twas an au – tumn night we raised the light on the old Head of Kin – sale.

It was a clear and cloudless night;
The wind blew steady and strong,
As gaily over the sparkling deep
Our good ship bowled along.
With the fiery foam beneath her bows
The white wave she did spread,
And bending alow her bosom in snow
She buried her lee cathead.

There was no talk of short'ning sail
By him who walked the poop,
And 'neath the press of her ponderous jib
The boom bent like a hoop;
And the groaning waterways told the strain
That held her stout main-tack,
But he only laughed as he gazed beaft
At the white and glist'ning track.

The mid-tide meets in the channel waves
That flow from shore to shore,
And the mist hung heavy along the land
From Featherstone to Dunmore,
And that sterling light on Tuskar Rock,
Where the old bell tolls each hour,
And the beacon light that shone so bright
Was quenched on Waterford tower.

What looms upon our starboard bow,
What hangs upon the breeze?
'Tis time our good ship hauled her wind
Abreast the old Saltees,
For by her ponderous press of sail
And by her stunted spars
We saw that our morning visitor
Was a British man-o'-war.

Up spake our noble Captain then
As a shot ahead of us passed:
"Haul snug your flowing courses!
Lay your topsails to the mast!"
Those Englishmen gave three loud hurrahs
From the deck of their covered ark,
And we answered back by a solid broadside
From the deck of our patriot bark.

"Out booms! Out booms!" our skipper cried:
"Out booms and give her sheet!"
For the swiftest keel that ever was launched
In all of the British fleet
Came pondering down upon us
With the white foam at her bow;
"Out booms! Out booms! and give her sheet!
Spare not your canvas now!"

But a swifter keel was 'neath our feet,
Nor did our sea-boys dread
When the star-spangled banner was hoisted;
To the mizzen peak was spread,
And amid a thundering shower of shot
With stunsails hoisting away,
Down the North Channel Paul Jones did steer
Just at the break of day.

The Constitution and the Guerrière

On June 18, 1812, at the urging of President James Madison, Congress declared war on Britain. On August 19, the U.S.S. *Constitution,* commanded by Captain Isaac Hull, defeated the British frigate *Guerrière* off the coast of Nova Scotia. It was the first American naval victory of the war.

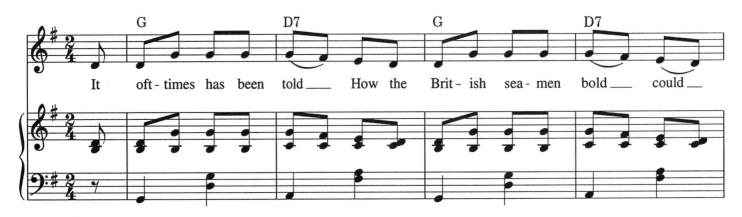

It oft-times has been told ___ How the Brit-ish sea-men bold ___ could ___

flog the tars of France so neat and han – dy oh! But they

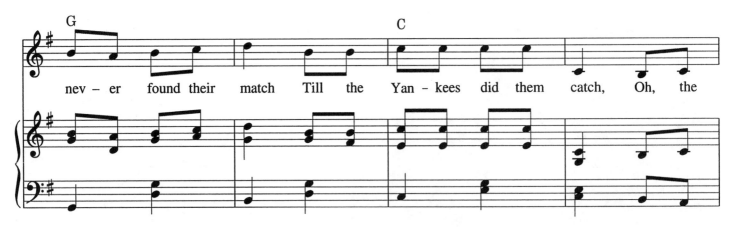

nev – er found their match Till the Yan-kees did them catch, Oh, the

Yan-kee boys for fight-ing are the dan – dy, oh!

The *Guerrière* so bold,
On the foaming ocean rolled,
Commanded proud Dacres the grandee, oh!
With as choice a British crew
As a rammer ever drew,
Could flog the Frenchmen two to one so handy, oh!

When this frigate hove in view,
Says proud Dacres to his crew,
"Come, clear ship for action and be handy, oh!
On the weather gage, boys, get her,"
And to make his men fight better,
He gave to them gunpowder mixed with brandy, oh!

Then Dacres loudly cries,
"Make this Yankee ship your prize,
You can in thirty minutes, neat and handy, oh!
Twenty-five's enough I'm sure,
And if you'll do it in a score,
I'll treat you to a double share of brandy, oh!"

The British shot flew hot,
Which the Yankees answered not,
Till they got within the distance they called handy, oh!
"Now," says Hull unto his crew,
"Boys, let's see what we can do,
If we take this boasting Briton we're the dandy, oh!"

The first broadside we poured
Took her mainmast by the board,
Which made this lofty frigate look abandon'd, oh!
Then Dacres shook his head;
To his officers he said,
"Lord! I didn't think those Yankees were so handy, oh!"

Our second told so well
That their fore and mizzen fell
Which dous'd the royal ensign neat and handy, oh!
"By George!" says he, "we're done,"
And they fired a lee gun,
While the Yankees struck up "Yankee Doodle Dandy," oh!

Then Dacres came on board
To deliver up his sword,
Which he was loath to lose, it was so handy, oh!
"Oh, keep your sword," says Hull,
"For it only makes you dull;
Cheer up and let us have a little brandy, oh!"

Now, fill your glasses full,
And we'll drink to Captain Hull,
And merrily we'll push about the brandy, oh!
John Bull may boast his fill,
But let the world say what it will,
The Yankee boys for fighting are the dandy, oh!

The Cumberland Crew

The next two songs celebrate the most important naval engagement of the Civil War, which took place on March 8, 1862. The Union sloop *Cumberland* was attacked and sunk by the iron-clad Confederate *Merrimac* in Chesapeake Bay. This battle marked the end of the era of wooden naval vessels. The military advantage to the Confederacy lasted but a day, as the Union launched its own iron-clad, *Monitor,* on March 9.

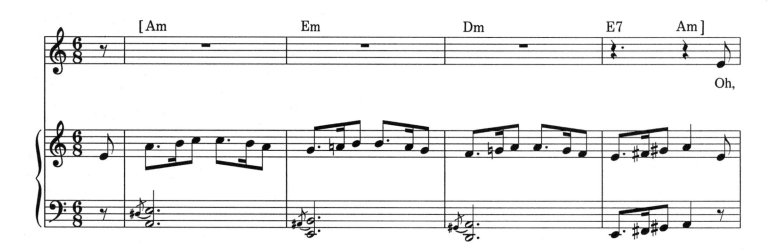

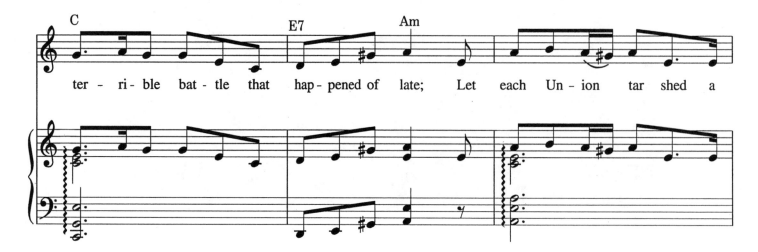

tear of sad pit - y When he thinks of the once gal - lant *Cum-ber - land's* fate. The

eighth day of March that told a ter - ri - ble sto - ry, When

man-y a brave tar to this world bid "a - dieu," Our flag____ was wrapped in a

man - tle of glo - ry by the he - ro - ic deeds of the *Cum -ber - land's* crew.

That ill-fated day, about ten in the morning,
The sky it was cloudless, and bright shone the sun;
The drums of the *Cumberland* sounded a warning
That told every man to stand by his gun.
When an iron-clad frigate down on us came bearing,
High up in the air her base Rebel flag flew;
An emblem of treason she proudly was wearing,
Determined to conquer the *Cumberland* crew.

They fought us three hours with stern resolution,
Till those Rebels found cannon could never decide;
For the flag of Secession had no power to quell them,
Though the blood from our scuppers did crimson the tide.
She struck us amidships, our planks she did sever,
Her sharp iron prow pierced our noble ship through;
And slowly we sank in Virginia's dark waters,
"We'll die by our guns," cried the *Cumberland* crew.

Oh, slowly she sank in the dark rolling waters,
Their voices on earth will be heard never more.
They'll be wept by Columbia's brave sons and fair daughters,
May their blood be avenged on Virginia's old shore.
And if ever sailors in battle assemble,
God bless our dear banner—the red, white, and blue;
Beneath its proud folds we'll cause tyrants to tremble,
Or sink at our guns like the *Cumberland* crew.

The Cumberland and the Merrimac

It was on last Mon-day morn-ing, _____ just at the break of day, _____ When the

good ship called *The Cum — ber - land* lay an - chored in her way, _____ And the

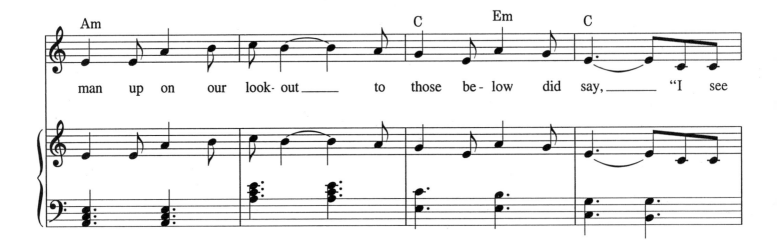

man up on our look- out _____ to those be - low did say, _____ "I see

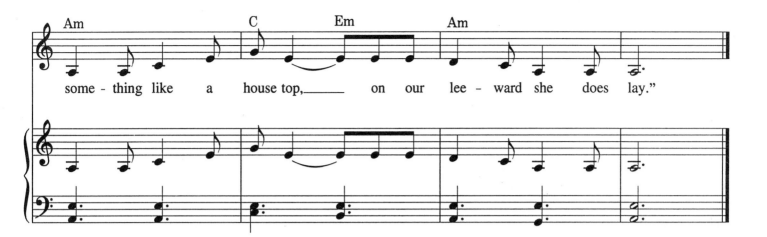

some - thing like a house top,_____ on our lee - ward she does lay."

Our captain seized his telescope and he gazed far o'er the blue,
And then he turned and spoke to his brave and loyal crew,
"That thing which yonder lies floating, that looks like some turtle's back,
It's that infernal Rebel steamer, and they call her *Merrimac.*"

Our decks were cleared for action and our guns were pointed through,
But still she kept a-coming up across the water blue,
And on, still on, she kept coming, till no distance stood apart;
When she sent a ball a-humming, stilled the beat of many a heart.

It was then we fired our broadside into her ribs of steel,
And yet no break in her iron made, no damage did she feel,
Till at length that Rebel pirate unto our captain spoke,
Saying, "Haul down your flying colors, now, or I'll sink your Yankee boat."

Our captain's eyes did glisten and his cheeks turned pale with rage,
And then in tones of thunder, to that Rebel pirate said:
"My men are brave and loyal, too, they're true to every man,
And before I'll strike my colors down, you may sink me in the sand."

Well, the *Merrimac* she left us then for a hundred yards or more,
Then with her whistles screaming out, on our wooden side she bore;
She struck us at our midship, and her ram went crashing through,
And the water came a-pouring in on our brave and loyal crew.

Well, our captain turned unto his men and unto them he did say,
"I never will strike my colors down while the *Cumberland* rides the wave,
But I'll go down with my gallant ship for to meet a watery grave,
And you, my loyal comrades, you may seek your lives to save."

They swore they never would leave him, but would man their guns afresh,
Poured broadside after broadside, till the water reached their breasts;
And then they sank far down, far down into the watery deep,
The Stars and Stripes still flying from her mainmast's highest peak.

Roll, Alabama, Roll

The Confederate gunboat *Alabama* was built in Birkenhead, England, in 1862. It was intended to counter the Union blockade of Confederate ports. For some two years it preyed upon Northern shipping, sinking and capturing some 56 merchant vessels. On June 19, 1865, the U.S.S. *Kearsarge* finally caught up with and sank the *Alabama* outside the French port of Cherbourg.

'Twas laid in the yard of Jonathan Laird,
  Roll, Alabama, roll.
'Twas laid in the town of Birkenhead,
  Roll, Alabama, roll.

Down the Mersey ways she rolled then,
  Roll, Alabama, roll.
Liverpool fitted her with guns and men,
  Roll, Alabama, roll.

From the Western Isles she sailed forth,
  Roll, Alabama, roll.
To destroy the commerce of the North,
  Roll, Alabama, roll.

To Cherbourg port she sailed one day,
  Roll, Alabama, roll.
To take her count of prize money,
  Roll, Alabama, roll.

Many a sailor lad he saw his doom,
  Roll, Alabama, roll.
When the *Ke-arsarge* it hove in view,
  Roll, Alabama, roll.

Till a ball from the forward pivot that day,
  Roll, Alabama, roll.
Shot the *Alabama's* stern away,
  Roll, Alabama, roll.

Off the three-mile limit in sixty-five,
  Roll, Alabama, roll.
The *Alabama* went to her grave,
  Roll, Alabama, roll.

Battleship of Maine

On the 15th of February, 1898, the U.S. battleship *Maine* was destroyed in Havana harbor by an explosion, with a loss of 260 lives. The cry of "Remember the *Maine!*" was taken up all across the United States. On the 20th of April, President McKinley approved a resolution demanding the withdrawal of Spain from its Cuban colony. On the 22nd, the President declared a blockage of Cuban ports. On the 24th, the Spanish government declared war—a war that would stretch from Cuba all the way to the Philippines.

Spain. When I get back from Spain I want to hon-or my name. It was all a-bout __ that Bat-tle-ship of Maine.

Why are you running,
Are you afraid to die?
The reason that I'm running,
Is because I cannot fly.
It was all about that Battleship of Maine. *Chorus*

The blood was a-running
And I was running too.
I give my feet good exercise,
I had nothing else to do.
It was all about that Battleship of Maine. *Chorus*

When they were a-chasing me,
I fell down on my knees.
First thing I cast my eyes upon
Was a great big pot of peas.
It was all about that Battleship of Maine. *Chorus*

The peas they was greasy,
The meat it was fat,
The boys was fighting Spaniards,
While I was fighting that.
It was all about that Battleship of Maine. *Chorus*

What kind of shoes
Do the rough riders wear?
Buttons on the side,
Cost five and a half a pair.
It was all about that Battleship of Maine. *Chorus*

What kind of shoes
Do the poor farmers wear?
Worn-out old brogans,
Cost a dollar a pair.
It was all about that Battleship of Maine. *Chorus*

Stung Right

Joe Hill (1879–1915) was the composer of dozens of militant labor and political songs during the early years of the 20th century. Here he takes ironic aim not only at the naive young man who joins the Navy "to see the world," but also at the Armour meat packing company, whose spoiled cans of meat supplied to U.S. forces were the cause of a notorious scandal during the Spanish–American War.

By Joe Hill

Stung right, stung right, E. Z. Mark, that's me. When my term is o - ver, and a - gain I'm free, There'll be no more trips a - round the world for me.

The man, he said, "The U.S. Fleet, it is no place for slaves,
For everything you have to do is stand and watch the waves!"
But in the morn, at five o'clock, they woke me from my snooze,
To scrub the deck and polish brass, and shine the captain's shoes! *Chorus*

One day a dude in uniform to me began to shout;
I simply plugged him in the jaw, and knocked him down and out;
They slammed me right in irons then and said, "You are a case."
On bread and water then I lived for twenty-seven days. *Chorus*

One day the captain said, "Today I'll show you something nice,
All hands line up, we'll go ashore and do some exercise."
He made us run for seven miles as fast as we could run, ·
And with a packing on our back that weighed a half a ton. *Chorus*

Some time ago when Uncle Sam he had a war with Spain,
And many of the boys in blue were in the battle slain,
Not all were killed by bullets, though; no, not by any means,
The biggest part that died were killed by Armour's Pork and Beans. *Chorus*

Heroes and
Hard Cases

Blow The Man Down

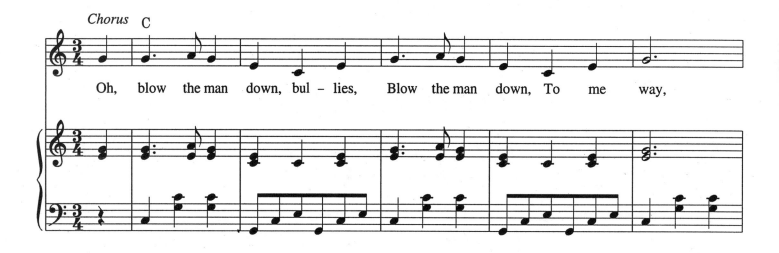

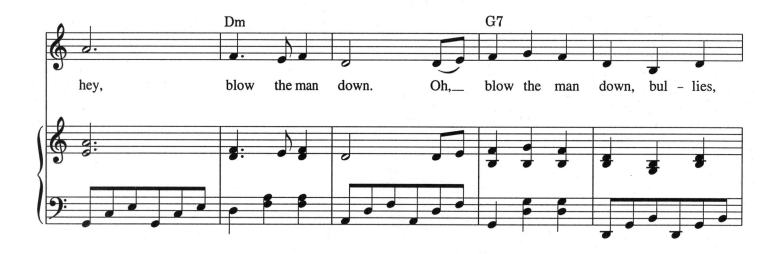

As I was a-walking down Paradise Street...
A pretty young damsel I chanced for to meet.... *Chorus*

She was round in the counter and bluff in the bow...
So I took in all sail and cried, "Way enough now!".... *Chorus*

I hailed her in English, she answered me clear...
"I'm from the *Black Arrow* bound to the *Shakespeare*".... *Chorus*

So I tailed her my flipper and took her in tow...
And yardarm to yardarm away we did go.... *Chorus*

And as we were going she said unto me...
"There's a spanking full-rigger just ready for sea".... *Chorus*

That spanking full-rigger for New York was bound...
She was very well manned and very well found.... *Chorus*

But as soon as that packet was clear of the bar...
The mate knocked me down with the end of a spar.... *Chorus*

And as soon as that packet was out on the sea...
'Twas dev'lish hard treatment of every degree.... *Chorus*

So I give you fair warning before we belay...
Don't never take heed of what pretty girls say.... *Chorus*

Reuben Ranzo

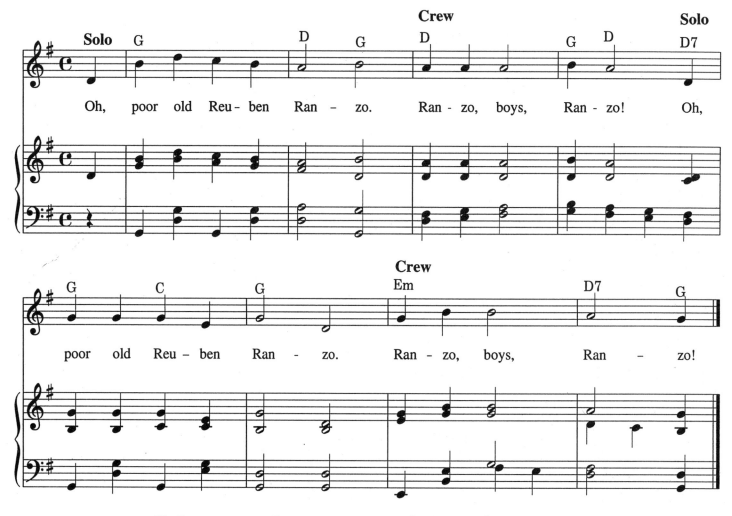

Oh, Ranzo was no sailor...
So he shipped aboard a whaler....

Oh, Ranzo was no beauty...
He couldn't do his duty....

So they took him to the gangway...
And gave him five-and-thirty....

And that was the end of Ranzo...
Oh, poor old Reuben Ranzo....

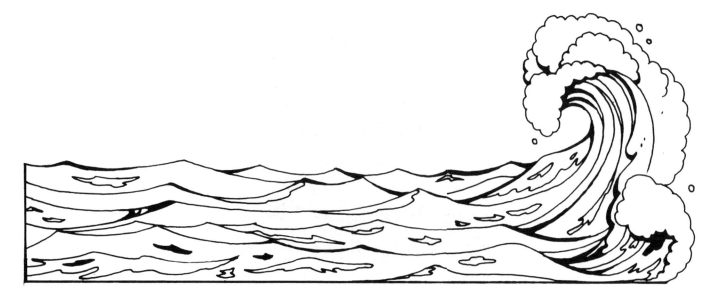

Pay Me My Money Down

Chorus

Pay me,— oh, pay me, — Pay me my mon-ey down, —

Pay me or go to jail, — Pay me my mon-ey down. _____

I thought I heard the captain say,
  Pay me my money down.
Tomorrow is our sailing day,
  Pay me my money down. *Chorus*

The very next day we sailed away,
  Pay me my money down.
We sailed the seas for a year and a day.
  Pay me my money down. *Chorus*

I wish I was Mister Howard's son,
  Pay me my money down.
Sit in the house and have all the fun,
  Pay me my money down. *Chorus*

I wish I was Mister Steven's son,
  Pay me my money down.
Sit in the shade and watch all the work done,
  Pay me my money down. *Chorus*

There's lots more verses to this song,
  Pay me my money down.
But I guess we'd better be moving along,
  Pay me my money down. *Chorus*

Fire Down Below

There is fire in the fore-top, fire in the main,
Fire in the windlass and fire in the chain. *Chorus*

There is fire in the fore-peak, fire down below,
Fire in the chain-plates, the bo'sun didn't know. *Chorus*

There is fire up aloft, there's fire down below,
Fire in the galley, the cook he didn't know. *Chorus*

Stormalong

Old Storm-y was a ___ fine old man. To me way, oh Storm-a -

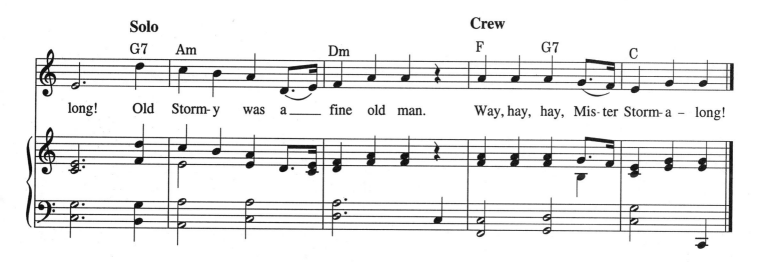

long! Old Storm-y was a ___ fine old man. Way, hay, hay, Mis-ter Storm-a – long!

Old Stormy he is dead and gone...
Oh, poor Stormy's dead and gone....

We'll dig his grave with a silver spade...
And lower him down with a golden chain....

I wish I was old Stormy's son...
I'd build me a ship of a thousand ton....

I'd sail this wide world round and round...
With plenty of money I'd be found....

I'd fill her up with New England rum...
And all my shellbacks they'd have some....

O Stormy's dead and gone to rest...
Of all the sailors he was the best....

Johnny Boker

Solo

Oh, do, my John-ny Bo - ker, Come rock and roll me

Crew

o - ver, Do, my John-ny Bo - ker, do!

Do, my Johnny Boker, the skipper is a rover....

Do, my Johnny Boker, the mate he's never sober....

Do, my Johnny Boker, the bo'sun is a tailor....

Do, my Johnny Boker, come roll me in the clover....

Whisky Johnny

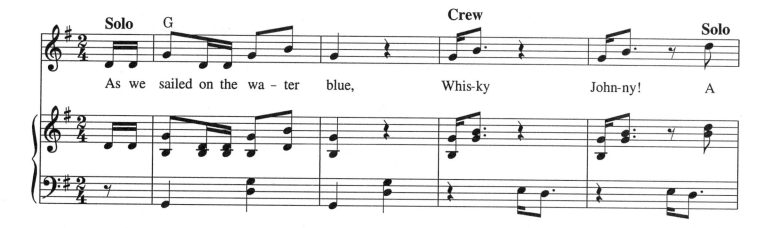

As we sailed on the wa – ter blue, Whis-ky John-ny!

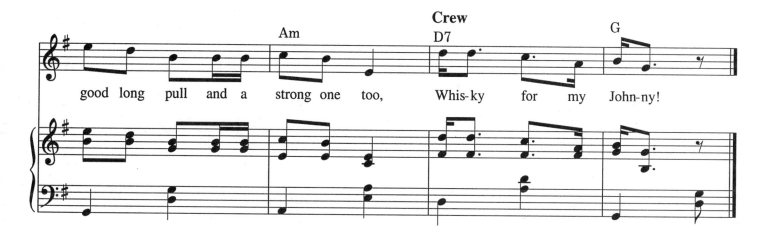

good long pull and a strong one too, Whis-ky for my John-ny!

Whisky killed my brother Tom...
I drink whisky all day long....

Whisky made me pawn my clothes...
Whisky gave me this red nose....

Whisky stole my brains away...
The bos'n pipes and I'll belay....

Whisky is the life of man...
Oh, I'll drink whisky while I can....

Oh, whisky straight and whisky strong...
Give me some whisky and I'll sing you a song....

Oh, whisky makes me wear old clothes...
Whisky gave me a broken nose....

Whisky killed my poor old dad...
Whisky drove my mother mad....

If whisky comes too near my nose...
I tip it up and down she goes....

I had a gal and her name was Lize...
She puts whisky in her pies....

My wife and I cannot agree...
She puts whisky in her tea....

Here comes the cook with a whisky can...
A glass of grog for every man....

A glass of grog for every man...
And a bottle full for the shanty-man....

I drink it hot and I drink it cold...
I drink it new and I drink it old....

Boney

While the British and French navies fought each other up and down the high seas for hundreds of years, the sailors of the warring fleets exchanged songs, verses, and phrases. Thus, the perennial "oh, my boys" of the British chanty emerged on the other side of the Channel as *"oh, mes boués."* This shanty about the rise and fall of Napoleon Bonaparte has its French counterpart as well:

C'est Jean-François de Nantes,
Oué, oué, oué.
Gabier de la *Fringante*
Oh, mes boués!
Jean-François.

Boney beat the Prooshians...
Boney beat the Rooshians....

Boney went to Moscow...
Moscow was a-blazing....

Boney went to Elba...
Boney he came back....

Boney went to Waterloo...
There he got his overthrow....

They took Boney off again...
'Board the *Billy Ruffian**....

Boney he was sent away...
'Way to St. He-len-i-ay....

Boney broke his heart and died...
Boney broke his heart and died....

*H.M.S. Bellerophon, the ship which carried Napoleon into exile.

What Shall We Do With The Drunken Sailor?

What shall we do with the drunk-en sail – or? What shall we do with the drunk- en sail – or?

What shall we do with the drunk-en sail - or? Ear - lye in the morn – ing.

Chorus:
Hooray, and up she rises,   (3)
Earlye in the morning.

Put him in the scuppers with a hose pipe on him....   (3)   *Chorus*

Heave him by the leg in a running bowline....   (3)   *Chorus*

Shave his belly with a rusty razor....   (3)   *Chorus*

That's what we'll do with the drunken sailor....   (3)   *Chorus*

Bound for
Distant Shores

South Australia

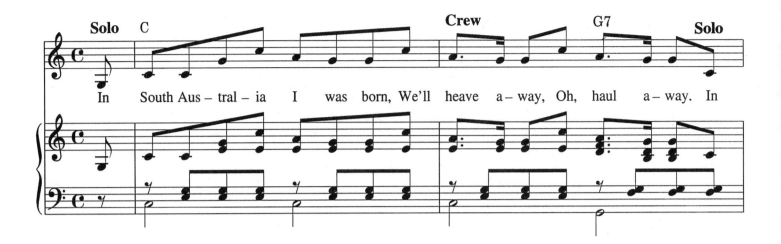

In South Aus – tral – ia I was born, We'll heave a – way, Oh, haul a – way. In

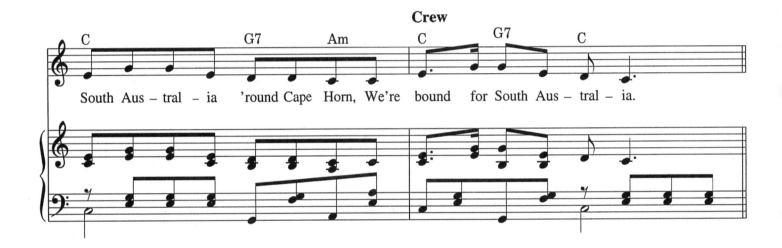

South Aus – tral – ia 'round Cape Horn, We're bound for South Aus – tral – ia.

Haul a – way you roll – ing kings, __ We'll heave a – way, haul a – way.

Haul a – way, We're bound to sing, __ We're bound for South Aus – tra – lia.

As I walked out one morning fair...
'Twas there I met Miss Nancy Blair.... *Chorus*

There ain't but one thing grieves my mind...
To leave Miss Nancy Blair behind.... *Chorus*

Oh, when I sailed across the sea...
My girl said she'd be true to me.... *Chorus*

I rung her all night, I rung her all day...
I rung her before we sailed away.... *Chorus*

Oh, when we lollop around Cape Horn...
You'll wish to God you'd never been born.... *Chorus*

I wish I was on Australia's strand...
With a glass of whisky in my hand.... *Chorus*

Get Up, Jack

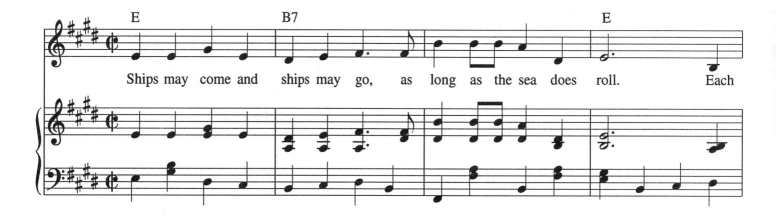

Ships may come and ships may go, as long as the sea does roll. Each

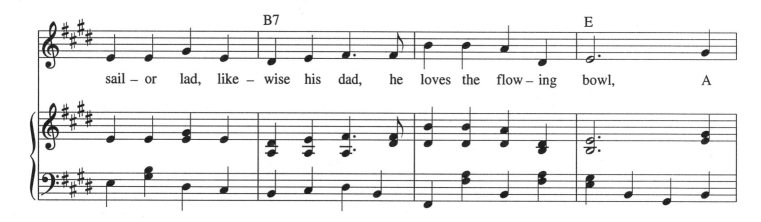

sail – or lad, like – wise his dad, he loves the flow – ing bowl, A

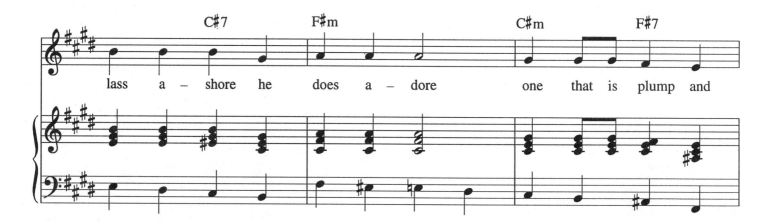

lass a – shore he does a – dore one that is plump and

round; But when his mon – ey is gone, it's the same old song: "Get

up, Jack! John, sit down!" Come a – long, come a – long, My

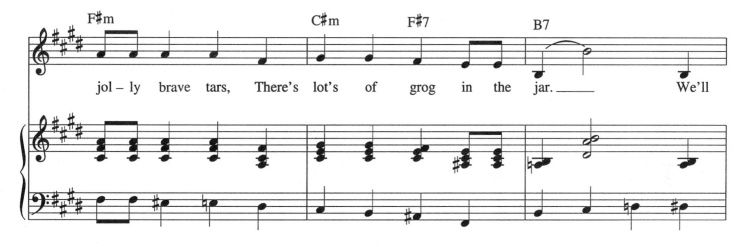

jol – ly brave tars, There's lot's of grog in the jar._____ We'll

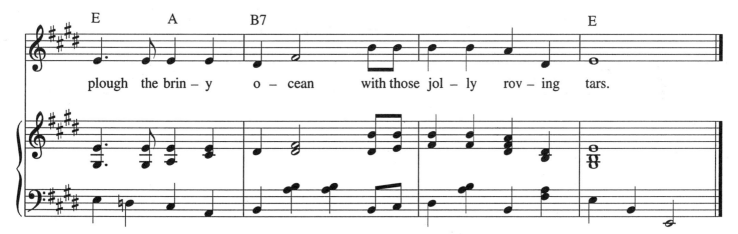

plough the brin – y o – cean with those jol – ly rov – ing tars.

When Jack's ashore, he beats his way to some boarding house,
He's welcomed in with rum and gin, likewise with port and souse,
He'll spend and spend and never offend, till he lies drunk on the ground,
But when his money is gone, it's the same old song:
"Get up, Jack! John, sit down!" *Chorus*

Now when Jack is old and weather-beaten, too old to knock about,
In some grogshop they'll let him stop, till eight bells he's turned out.
Then he cries and he sighs right up to the skies: "Good Lord, I'm homeward bound."
For when your money is gone, it's the same old song:
"Get up, Jack! John, sit down!" *Chorus*

The Dom Pedro

It's of a flash pack-et, a pack-et of fame. She be-longs to New York and *Dom Pe-dro's* her name. She's rammed up and jammed up on deck and be-low; We're bound for Shang-hai in the *Dom Pe-de-ro.* Sing-ing down, down, down der-ry down.

Now the pilot came down and these words he did say,
"Get ready, me boys, the ship's going away."
We braced up our yards and we gave her the slip,
And it's down Boston harbor that packet did rip. *Chorus*

Oh, it's now we are sailing down off of Cape Cod,
Where many a hard flashy packet has trod;
The wind it breezed up and the water did boil,
And at eight bells that night we clewed up our main royal. *Chorus*

And now we are sailing down on to the Line;
We catched all the rain-water, we had plenty of time;
We filled up our casks, as you now plainly see,
And then shaped our course for the port of Shanghai. *Chorus*

Now the captain is aft and he's reading a book;
He'll come for'ard bimeby and he'll growl at the cook;
He will lift up his eyes to the blessings of God
Over a plate of boiled rice and some rusty salt cod. *Chorus*

It's now we're arrived in the port of Shanghai;
We'll go ashore, shipmates, strange faces to see.
We'll lay up aloft and we'll furl all our sails,
Excepting the spanker that hangs in the brails. *Chorus*

Now our cargo's discharged and we are taking in;
We're expecting to go back to Boston ag'in;
And when we get there so jolly we'll be,
We'll be twenty merry sports all the way from Shanghai. *Chorus*

The Banks Of Newfoundland

You ram-blin' boys of Liv-er-pool, I'll have ye's to be - ware,_____ When you

go in a Yan - kee pack - et ship no _ dun - ga-rees do wear,_____ But _

have a mon - key jack-et all _ un - to your com - mand,_____ For there

blows some cold nor' - wes - ters on the Banks of New- found-land._____ We'll

wash her and we'll scrub her down with ho – ly–stone and_ sand, _____ And we'll

bid a – dieu to the Vir – gin Rocks on the Banks of New – found-land. _____

As I lay in my bunk one night, a-dreaming all alone,
I dreamt I was in Liverpool, way up in Marrowbone
With my true-love beside me and a jug of ale in hand,
When I woke quite broken-hearted on the Banks of Newfoundland. *Chorus*

We had one Lynch from Ballinahinch, Jimmy Murphy and Mike Moore;
It was in the winter of seventy-two those sea-boys suffered sore.
They pawned their clothes in Liverpool and sold them all out of hand,
For she could not see the sea-boys freeze on the Banks of Newfoundland. *Chorus*

Now, boys, we're off Sandy Hook, and the land's all covered with snow;
We'll pass the tugboat our hawser and for New York we will tow,
And when we arrive at the Black Ball dock the boys and the girls will stand;
We'll bid adieu to packet-sailing and the Banks of Newfoundland.

Last Chorus:
We'll wash her and we'll scrub her out with holystone and sand,
For it's whilst we're here we can't be there, on the Banks of Newfoundland!

The Dreadnaught

There is a flash pack – et, flash pack – et of fame, She hails from New York and the *Dread-nought's* her name. She is bound to the west – ward, where the storm – y winds blow. Bound a – way in the *Dread-naught* to the west - ward we'll go.

Now the *Dreadnaught* is hauling out of Waterloo dock,
Where the boys and the girls to the pierhead do flock.
They give her three cheers, as the tears down do flow,
Crying, "God bless the *Dreadnaught* where'er she may go!"

Now the *Dreadnaught* she lies in the river Mersey,
A-waiting the tugboat to take her to sea,
Out around the Rock Light where the salt tides do flow,
Bound away to the westward in the *Dreadnaught* we'll go.

Now the *Dreadnaught's* a-howling down the wild Irish Sea,
Her passengers merry, with hearts full of glee;
Her sailors like lions walk the deck to and fro;
She's the Liverpool packet—O Lord, let her go!

Now the *Dreadnaught* is sailing the Atlantic so wide,
Where the high roaring seas roll along her black side,
With her sails tautly set for the Red Cross to show
She's the Liverpool packet—O Lord, let her go!

Now the *Dreadnaught* is crossing the banks of Newfoundland,
Where the water's so green and the bottom's all sand,
Where the fishes of the ocean they swim to and fro,
She's the Liverpool packet—O Lord, let her go!

And now she is sailing down the Long Island shore,
Where the pilot will board us as he's oft done before.
"Fill away your main-topsail, board your main-tack also!"
She's the Liverpool packet—O Lord, let her go!

Now the *Dreadnaught's* arriv-ed in New York once more.
Let's go ashore, shipmates, on the land we adore,
With wives and with sweethearts so happy we'll be,
And drink to the *Dreadnaught* wherever we be.

Now a health to the *Dreadnaught* and all her brave crew,
To bold Captain Samuels and his officers too;
Talk about your flash packets, *Swallowtail* and *Black Ball,*
The *Dreadnaught's* the flier that outsails them all.

From Boston Harbor We Set Sail

From Bos – ton har – bor we set sail, When it was blow – ing a

dev – il of a gale, With our ring – tail set all a – baft the miz – zen peak, And our

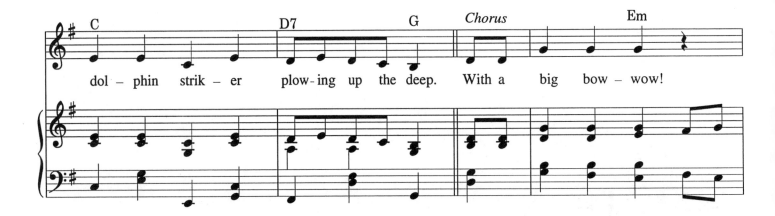

dol – phin strik – er plow – ing up the deep. With a big bow – wow!

Tow – row – row! Fol – di rol – de ri – do – day!

Up comes the skipper from down below,
And he looks aloft and he looks alow,
And he looks alow and he looks aloft,
And it's "Coil up your ropes there, fore and aft." *Chorus*

Then down to his cabin he quickly crawls,
And unto his steward he loudly bawls,
"Go mix me a glass that will make me cough,
For it's better weather here than it is up aloft." *Chorus*

We poor sailors standing on the deck,
With the blasted rain all a-pouring down our necks;
Not a drop of grog would he to us afford,
But he damns our eyes with every other word. *Chorus*

And one thing which we have to crave
Is that he may have a watery grave,
So we'll heave him down into some dark hole,
Where the sharks'll have his body and the devil have his soul. *Chorus*

The Jamestown Homeward Bound

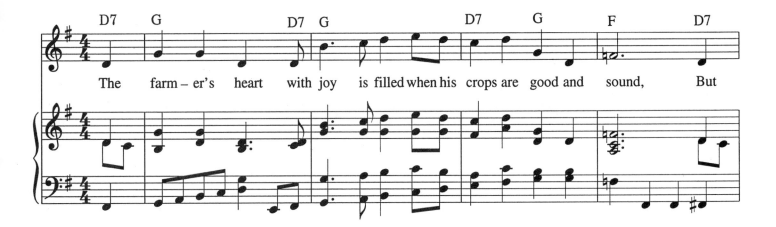

The farm-er's heart with joy is filled when his crops are good and sound, But

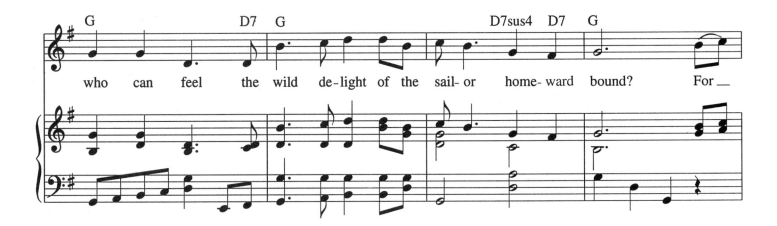

who can feel the wild de-light of the sail-or home-ward bound? For __

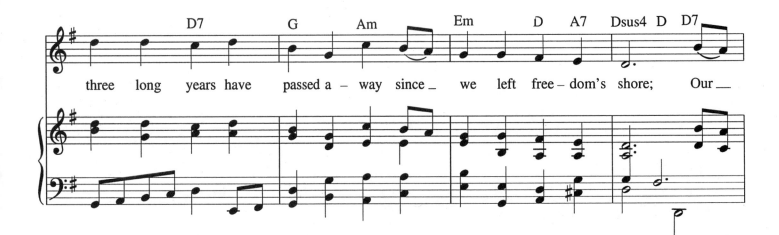

three long years have passed a — way since __ we left free-dom's shore; Our __

long – felt   wish has   come at   last, and we're home – ward bound once - more.

Chorus (sung to last 8 measures of verse, repeated):
To where the sky is as clear as the maiden's eye who longs for our return,
To the land where milk and honey flows and liberty it was born.
So fill our sails with the favoring gales, and with shipmates all around,
We'll give three cheers for our starry flag and the *Jamestown* homeward bound.

To the Mediterranean shores we've been, and its beauties we have seen,
And Sicily's grand and lofty hills and Italy's gardens green,
We've gazed on Mount Vesuvius, with its rugged slumbering dome;
Night is the time in that red clime when the sailor thinks of home. *Chorus*

We've strayed round Pompeii's ruined wall, and on them carved our names,
And thought of its ancient beauties past and vanished lordly dames,
And gazed on tombs of mighty kings who oft in battle won,
But what were they all in their sway with our brave Washington? *Chorus*

And now we have arrived in port and stripping's our last job,
And friendly faces look around in search of Bill or Bob.
They see that we are safe at last from the perils of the sea,
Saying, "You're welcome, Columbia's mariners, to your homes and liberty." *Chorus*

Cape Cod Girls

O, Cape Cod boys they have no sleds...
They slide downhill on codfish heads.... *Chorus*

O, Cape Cod cats they have no tails...
They blew away in heavy gales.... *Chorus*

Leave Her, Johnny

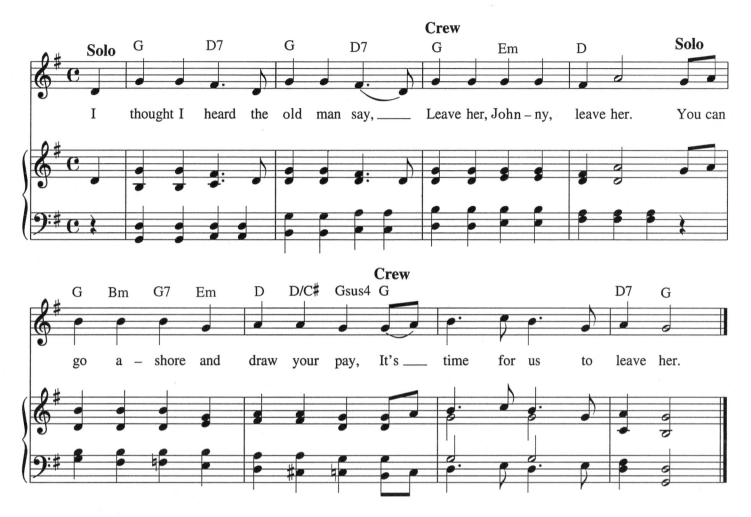

Solo I thought I heard the old man say, ___ Leave her, John–ny, leave her. You can go a – shore and draw your pay, It's ___ time for us to leave her.

You may make her fast and pack your gear...
And leave her moored to the West Street pier....

The winds were foul, the work was hard...
From Liverpool docks to the Brooklyn yard....

She would neither steer nor wear nor stay...
She shipped it green both night and day....

She shipped it green and she made us curse...
The mate is a devil and the old man worse....

The winds were foul, the ship was slow...
The grub was bad, the wages low....

The winds were foul, the trip was long...
But before we go we'll sing this song....

One More Day

We're homeward bound tomorrow, Johnny...
We leave you without sorrow.... *Chorus*

Can't you hear the old man snarling, Johnny?...
Can't you hear the capstan pawling?.... *Chorus*

Oh, heave and sight the anchor, Johnny...
Oh, heave and sight the anchor.... *Chorus*

I'm bound away to leave you, Johnny...
But I will not deceive you.... *Chorus*

Blow, Boys, Blow

How do you know she's a Yankee liner?...
The Stars and Stripes float out behind her....

How do you know she's a Yankee packet?...
They fired a gun, I heard the racket....

And who d'you think is the captain of her?...
Why, Bully Hayes is the captain of her....

Oh, Bully Hayes, he loves us sailors...
Yes, he does like hell and blazes!....

And who d'you think is the mate aboard her?...
Santander James is the mate aboard her....

Santander James, he's a rocker from hell, boys...
He'll ride you down as you ride the spanker....

And what d'you think they've got for dinner?...
Pickled eels' feet and bullock's liver....

Then blow, my bullies, all together...
Blow, my boys, for better weather....

Blow, boys, blow, the sun's drawing water...
Three cheers for the cook and one for his daughter....

51

The Sloop John B.

I feel so break up, _____ I want to go home. _____

Chorus:
So hoist up the *John B.* sails,
See how the mainsail sets,
Send for the captain ashore, let me go home.
Let me go home, let me go home,
I feel so break up, I want to go home.

The first mate, oh, he got drunk,
Broke up the people's trunk,
Constable had to come and take him away.
Sheriff Johnstone, please leave me alone,
I feel so break-up, I want to go home. *Chorus*

The poor cook, oh, he got fits,
Ate up all of the grits.
Then he took and threw away all of the corn.
Sheriff Johnstone, please leave me alone,
This is the worst trip I ever been on. *Chorus*

Santy Anno

In the years following the Mexican War, songs concerning the defeated Mexican general, Santa Ana, began to appear in American and British sea chanteys.

We're sail-ing down the riv-er from Liv-er — pool Heave a —

way, San — ty An-no! _____ A — round Cape Horn to

Fris — co Bay, All __ on the plains of Mex — i — co.

Chorus:
So heave her up and away we'll go,
Heave away, Santy Anno;
Heave her up and away we'll go,
All on the plains of Mexico.

When Zachary Taylor gained the day,
Heave away, Santy Anno,
He made poor Santy run away,
All on the plains of Mexico. *Chorus*

She's a fast clipper ship and a bully good crew,
Heave away, Santy Anno,
A down-East Yankee for her captain, too.
All on the plains of Mexico. *Chorus*

There's plenty of gold so I've been told,
Heave away, Santy Anno,
There's plenty of gold so I've been told
Way out West to Californi-o. *Chorus*

Back in the days of forty-nine,
Heave away, Santy Anno,
Those are the days of the good old times,
All on the plains of Mexico. *Chorus*

General Scott and Taylor, too,
Heave away, Santy Anno,
Made poor Santy meet his Waterloo,
All on the plains of Mexico. *Chorus*

When I leave the ship, I will settle down,
Heave away, Santy Anno,
And marry a girl named Sally Brown,
All on the plains of Mexico. *Chorus*

Santy Anno was a good old man,
Heave away, Santy Anno,
Till he got into war with your Uncle Sam,
All on the plains of Mexico. *Chorus*

Banks Of The Sacramento

In 1849 there were two ways to get from the East Coast to the gold fields of California: overland by covered wagon across the Great Plains, the desert, and the high Sierras; or by water around Cape Horn. Either way you might make it—or you might not. The clipper ship was born in 1851. The swiftest ship afloat was the *Flying Cloud*—New York to San Francisco in 89 days and 20 hours. That was something to sing about!

Words: Traditional
Music: Stephen Foster, Camptown Races

plen–ty of gold, so I've been told, On the banks of the Sac – ra – – men – to.

O we were the boys to make her go...
Around Cape Horn in the frost and snow.... *Chorus*

Around Cape Stiff in seventy days...
Around Cape Stiff is a mighty long ways.... *Chorus*

When we was tacking 'round Cape Horn...
I often wished I'd a never been born.... *Chorus*

O the mate he whacked me around and around...
And I wished I was home all safe and sound.... *Chorus*

O when we got to the Frisco docks...
The girls all were in their Sunday frocks.... *Chorus*

Deep Sea Blues

An American soldier's impression of life on a troop ship headed for France in World War I.

Words traditional
Music by Jerry Silverman

Oh, all day long I'm look – in' for trees, Look – in' for sand, look – in' for land, 'Cause I've got those aw – ful weep – in', sleep – in', Got those

Ten Thousand Miles Away

"At a time when the British statute-book bristled with capital felonies, when then the pickpocket or sheep-stealer was hanged out of hand, when Sir Samuel Romilly... declared that the laws of England were written in blood, another and less sanguinary penalty came into great favour. The deportation of criminals beyond the seas...the 'first fleet' of Australian annals reached Botany Bay in January 1788...." (*Encyclopedia Britannica,* 1911 edition)

Sing I for a brave and a gal – lant barque, and a stiff and a

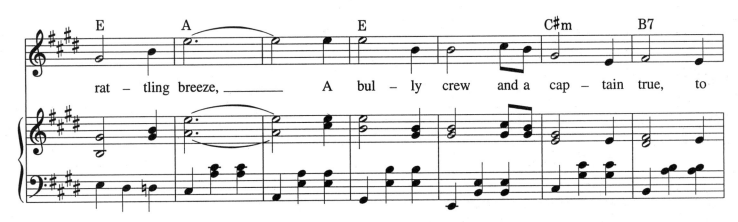

rat – tling breeze, A bul – ly crew and a cap – tain true, to

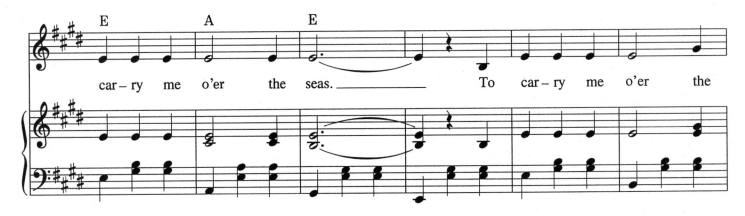

car – ry me o'er the seas. To car – ry me o'er the

seas, my boys, to my true love so gay – ay – ay, Who

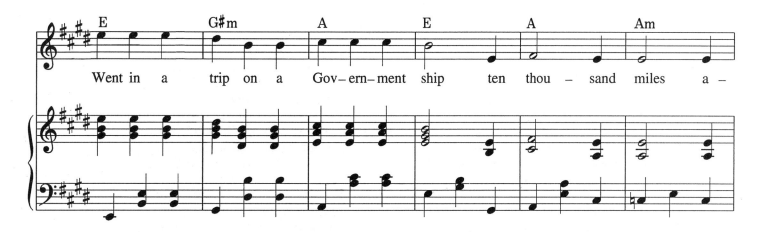

Went in a trip on a Gov—ern—ment ship ten thou—sand miles a—

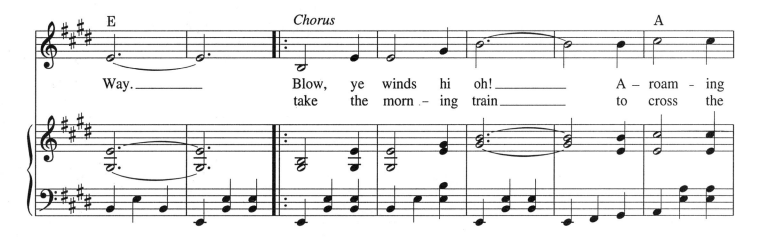

Chorus

Way. Blow, ye winds hi oh! A—roam—ing
take the morn—ing train to cross the

I will go; I'll stay no more on Eng—land's
rag—ing main, I'm on the road to my true

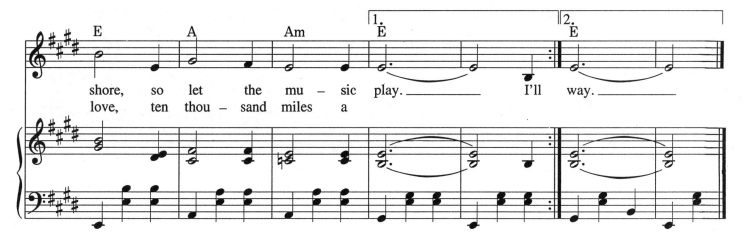

shore, so let the mu—sic play. I'll way.
love, ten thou—sand miles a

My true love she was handsome,
My true love she was young,
Her eyes were blue as the violet's hue,
And silvery was the sound of her tongue;
And silvery was the sound of her tongue, my boys,
And, while I sing this lay-ay-ay,
She's a-doing of the grand in a far-off land,
Ten thousand miles away! *Chorus*

Dark and dismal was the day
When last I seen my Meg,
She's a Government band around each hand,
And another one round her leg;
And another one round her leg, my boys,
As the big ship left the bay-ay-ay,
Adieu, said she, remember me,
Ten thousand miles away! *Chorus*

Oh! if I were a sailor lad,
Or even a bombardier,
I'd hire a boat and go afloat,
And straight to my true love steer;
And straight to my true love steer, my boys,
Where the dancing dolphins play-ay-ay,
And the whales and sharks kick up their larks,
Ten thousand miles away! *Chorus*

The sun may shine through a London fog,
Or the river run bright and clear,
The ocean's brine be changed to wine,
And I forget my beer,
And I forget my beer, my boys,
Or the landlord's quarter day-ay-ay,
But never will part from my own sweetheart
Ten thousand miles away. *Chorus*

Love 'Em and Leave 'Em

The Eddystone Light

The Eddystone rocks lie about 14 miles off Plymouth. Four lighthouses have been constructed on these rocks: Winstanley's Tower, completed in 1698 and swept away in November 1703; Ruyard's Tower, completed in 1709 and destroyed by fire in 1755; Smeaton's Tower, completed in 1759 and dismantled when the Douglass Tower was completed in 1882. Probably the keeper in question exercised his functions either in the latter years of the Smeaton Tower or the early years of the Douglass Tower.

My fath – er was the keep – er of the Ed – dy – stone Light, And he slept with a mer – maid one fine night. From this un – ion there came three: Two lit – tle fish – es and the oth – er was me.

Yo ho ho, the wind blows free. Oh, for the life on the roll – ing sea.

One night as I was a-trimming of the glim,
And a-singing a verse from the evening hymn,
A voice from the starboard shouted, "Ahoy!"
And there was my mother a-sitting on a buoy. *Chorus*

"Oh, what has become of my children three?"
My mother then she said to me.
"One was exhibited as a talking fish,
And the other was served on a chafing dish." *Chorus*

Then the phosphorus flashed in her seaweed hair,
I looked again and my mother wasn't there.
But a voice came echoing out through the night,
"To hell with the keeper of the Eddystone Light!" *Chorus*

The Fireship

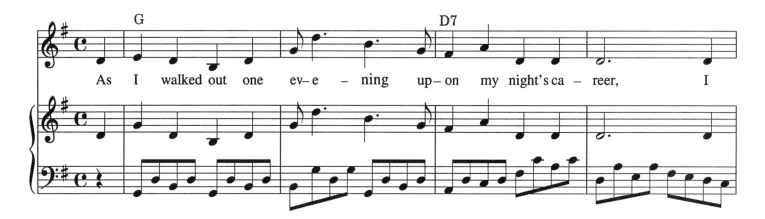

As I walked out one ev–e – ning up–on my night's ca – reer, I

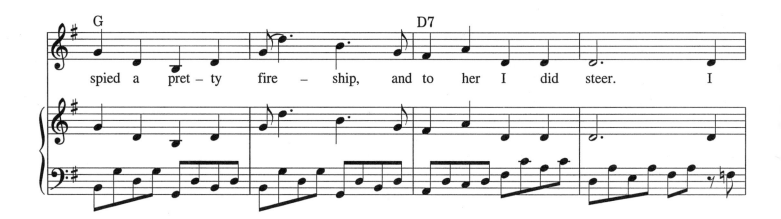

spied a pret–ty fire – ship, and to her I did steer. I

hoist – ed up my sig–a–nal, which she did quick–ly view; —— And

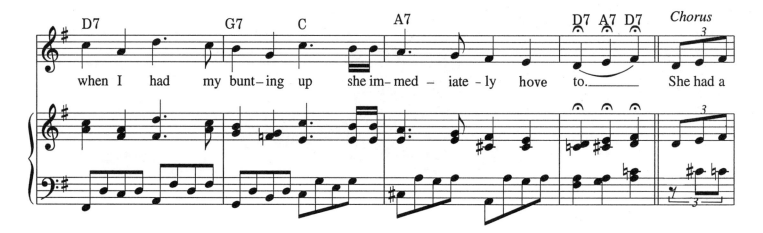

when I had my bunt–ing up she im–med – iate – ly hove to.———— She had a

dark and a rov–ing eye,_____ And her hair hung down in ring–o–lets;_____ A nice girl, a de–cent girl, But one of the rak–ish kind.

"Excuse me, sir," she said to me, "for being out so late.
For if my parents knew of this, then sad would be my fate.
My father is a minister—a good and virtuous man.
My mother is a Methodist—I do the best I can." *Chorus*

I took her to a tav–er–in and treated her with wine.
Oh, little did I ever think she was the rakish kind.
I handled her, I dandled her—but much to my surprise,
She was only an old pirate ship rigged up in a disguise. *Chorus*

So listen, all you sailor men, who sail upon the sea,
Beware of them there fireships—one was the ruin of me.
Beware of them, stay clear of them—they'll be the ruin of you;
'Twas there I had my mizzen sprung and my strong-box broken through. *Chorus*

The Girls Around Cape Horn

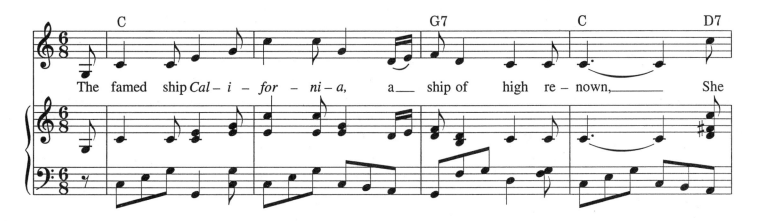

The famed ship Cal – i – for – ni – a, a__ ship of high re – nown,_____ She

lay in Bos – ton har – bor, long–side of that pret–ty town,_____ A –

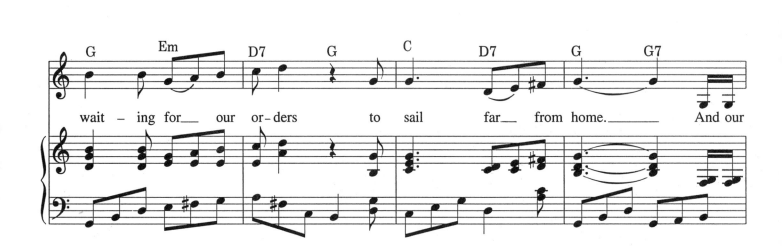

wait – ing for__ our or– ders to sail far__ from home._____ And our

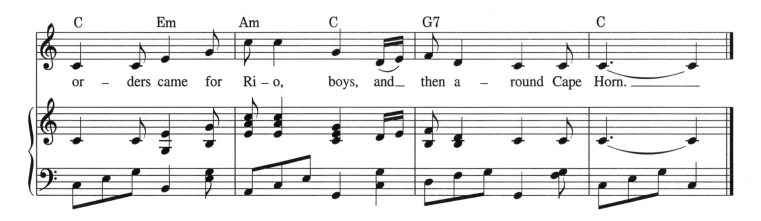

or – ders came for Ri – o, boys, and__ then a – round Cape Horn._____

When we arrived in Rio we lay there quite a while,
A-fixing up our rigging and bending our new sails.
From ship to ship they cheered us as we did sail along,
And they wished us pleasant weather while rounding of Cape Horn.

While rounding of Cape Horn, my boys, fair nights and pleasant days.
Next place we dropped our anchor was in Valparaiso Bay,
Where those Spanish girls they did roll down, I solemnly do swear
They far excel those Yankee girls with their dark and wavy hair.

They love a Yankee sailor when he goes on a spree;
He'll dance and sing and make things ring, and his money he will spend free,
And when his money it is all gone, on him they won't impose;
They far excel those Liverpool girls who will pawn and steal his clothes.

Here's a health to Valparaiso along the Chile main,
Likewise to those Peruvian girls, they treated me so fine.
If ever I live to get paid off, I'll sit and drink till morn
A health to the dashing Spanish girls I met around Cape Horn.

A-Roving

A – rov – ing a – rov – ing, Since rov–ing's been my – ru – i – in. I'll

go no more a – rov – ing with you fair maid.

I took this fair maid for a walk...
And we had such a loving talk.... *Chorus*

And didn't I tell her stories, too...
Of the gold we found in Timbuctoo.... *Chorus*

She swore that she'd be true to me...
But spent my money fast and free.... *Chorus*

Now scarce had I been gone to sea...
When a soldier took her on his knee.... *Chorus*

'Round The Bay Of Mexico

Then, 'round the Bay of Mex–i–co,__ Way oh, Su – si–an–na.

Mex–i–co – is the place that I be–long in. 'Round the Bay of Mex–i–co.__

When I was a young man in my prime...
I'd love those pretty girls two at a time....

The reason those girls they love me so...
Because I don't tell everything that I know....

Them Nassau girls ain't got no combs...
They comb their hair with whipper-back bones....

Sally Brown

She had a farm in the isle of Jamaicer...
Where she raised sugar cane and tobaccer....

Also she had a fine young daughter...
And that's the gal that I was arter....

For seven long years I courted Sally...
And when I asked her if she'd marry....

These lily-white hands and slender wais'...
A tarry sailor will ne'er embrace....

So then she married a Cuban soldier...
Who beat her up and stole her money....

One night she was taken with a pain in her belly...
And they sent for the doctor whose name was Kelly....

And from her took a little baby...
O Sally dear, why didn't you have me?....

Mary-Anne

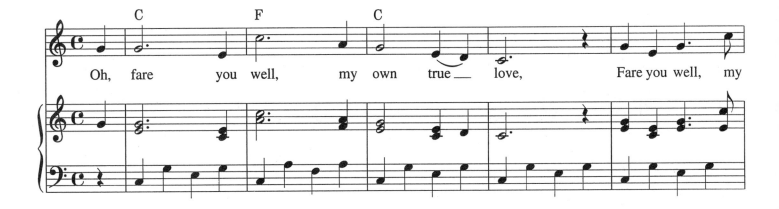

Oh, fare you well, my own true __ love, Fare you well, my

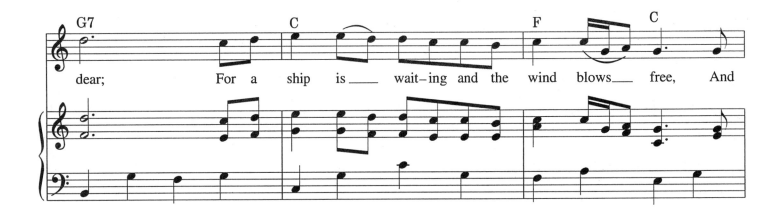

dear; For a ship is __ wait-ing and the wind blows__ free, And

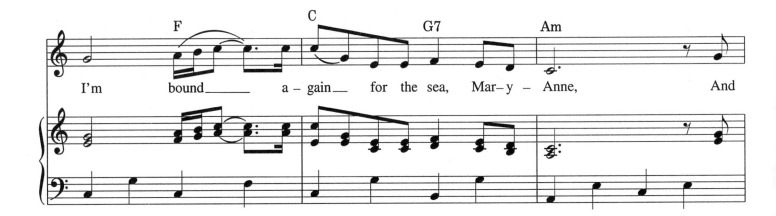

I'm bound_____ a – gain__ for the sea, Mar–y – Anne, And

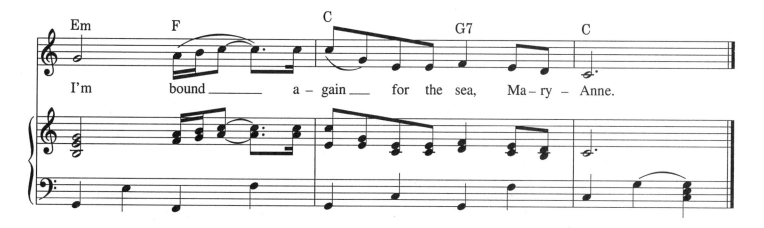

I'm bound a – gain for the sea, Ma – ry – Anne.

Oh don't you see the little dove, setting on a pine
Mourning the loss of her own true love
As I will mourn for mine, my dear Mary-Anne. (2)

The lobster boilin' in the pot, and the crayfish on the line,
They're suffering long but it's nothing like
The ache I bear for thee, my dear Mary-Anne. (2)

Oh had I but a flask of gin, and sugar here for two,
And a great big bowl for to mix it in,
I would mix a drink for you, my dear Mary-Anne. (2)

Can't You Dance The Polka?

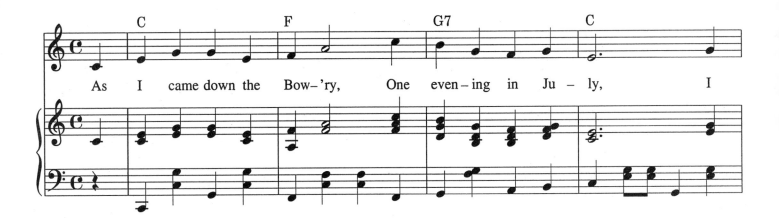

As I came down the Bow–'ry, One even – ing in Ju – ly, I

met a maid who asked my trade, And a sail – or John, said I.___ Then a –

way, you San – ty, My dear An – nie, Oh, you

New York girls, Can't you dance the pol-ka?

To Tiffany's I took her, I did not mind expense,
I bought her two gold earrings—they cost me fifty cents. *Chorus*

Says she, "You lime-juice sailor, now see me home you may."
But when we reached her cottage door she unto me did say. *Chorus*

"My young man he's a sailor, with his hair cut short behind;
He wears a tarry jumper, and he sails the Black Ball line." *Chorus*

Sailor On The Deep Blue Sea

It was— on one sum – mer's even – ing. Just a – bout the hour — of

three, When my dar – ling start–ed to leave me, For to sail up– on the deep blue— sea.

Oh, he promised to write me a letter,
He said he'd write to me;
But I've not heard from my darling,
Who is sailing on the deep blue sea.

Oh, my mother's dead and buried,
My pa's forsaken me;
And I have no one for to love me,
But the sailor on the deep blue sea.

Farewell to friends and relations,
It's the last you'll see of me;
For I'm going to end my troubles,
By drowning in the deep blue sea.

Johnny Todd

Johnny Todd, he went a sailing, For to cross the ocean wide.

But he left his true love behind him, Walking by the Liverpool tide.

For a week she wept full sorely,
Tore her hair and wrung her hands,
Till she met with another sailor
Walking on the Liverpool sands.

Oh fair maid, why are you weeping
For your Johnny gone to sea?
If you'll wed with me tomorrow
I will kind and constant be.

I will buy you sheets and blankets,
I'll buy you a wedding ring;
You shall have a silver cradle
For to rock the baby in.

Johnny Todd came home from sailing,
Sailing o'er the ocean wide;
But he found that his fair and false one
Was another sailor's bride.

Now young men who go a-sailing,
For to fight the foreign foe;
Do not leave your love like Johnny,
Marry her before you go.

The Handsome Cabin Boy

The story of the woman who dons men's clothes and goes to sea is a favorite in British sea-song tradition. Perhaps a few such occurrences inspired ballad-makers to expand on the almost limitless possibilities of the theme. This version of the song is somewhat unusual due to the presence of the captain's wife—leading one to suspect that she was written into the song to provide some justification for the captain's philandering.

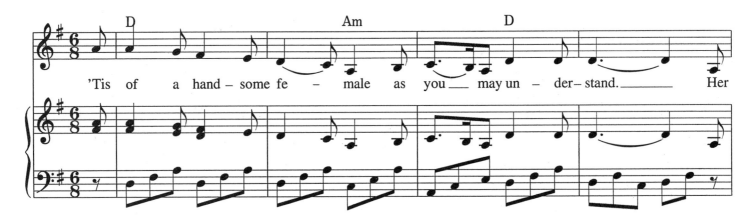

'Tis of a hand – some fe – male as you __ may un – der–stand. ____ Her

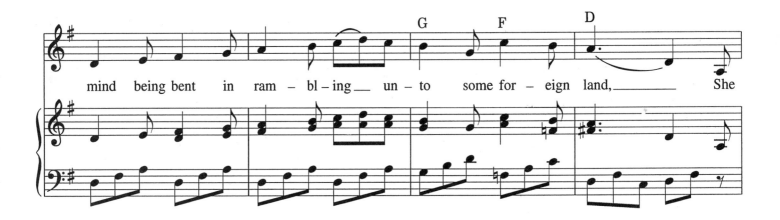

mind being bent in ram – bl – ing __ un – to some for – eign land, _____ She

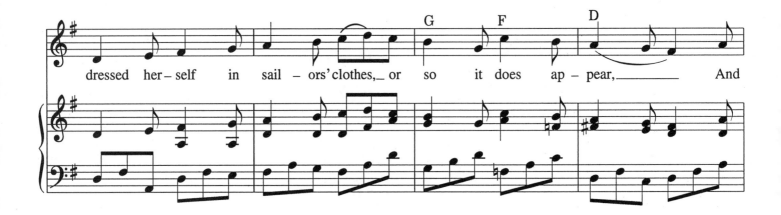

dressed her–self in sail – ors' clothes,_ or so it does ap–pear, _____ And

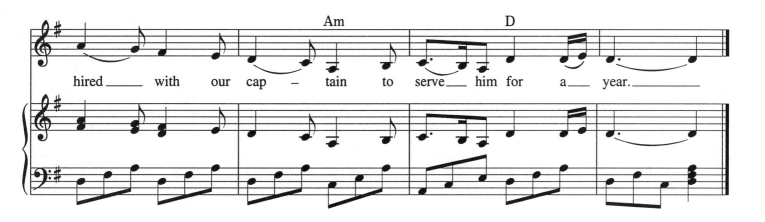

hired _____ with our cap – tain to serve ___ him for a ___ year._____

The captain's wife she being on board, she seem-ed in great joy,
To see her husband had engaged such a handsome cabin boy,
And now and then she'd slip in a kiss and she would have liked to toy,
But the captain found the secret of the handsome cabin boy.

Her cheeks were red and rosy and her hair hung in its curls,
The sailors often smiled and said he looks just like a girl.
But eating the captain's biscuits, their color didn't destroy,
And the waist did swell on pretty Nell, the handsome cabin boy.

'Twas in the Bay of Biscay our gallant ship did plow,
One night among the sailors was a fearful scurrying row,
They tumbled from their hammocks for their sleep it did destroy,
And swore about the groaning of the handsome cabin boy.

Oh, doctor, oh dear doctor, the cabin boy did cry,
My time has come, I am undone and I must surely die.
The doctor come a-running and smiled at the fun,
To think a sailor lad should have a daughter or a son.

The sailors when they heard the joke, they all did stand and stare,
The child belonged to none of them they solemnly did swear.
The captain's wife she looked at him and said, "I wish you joy,
For it's either you or I betrayed the handsome cabin boy."

Then each man took his tot of rum, and drunk success to trade,
And likewise to the cabin boy who was neither man nor maid.
Here's hopin' the wars don't rise again, our sailors to destroy,
And here's hoping for a jolly lot more like the handsome cabin boy.

81

John Riley

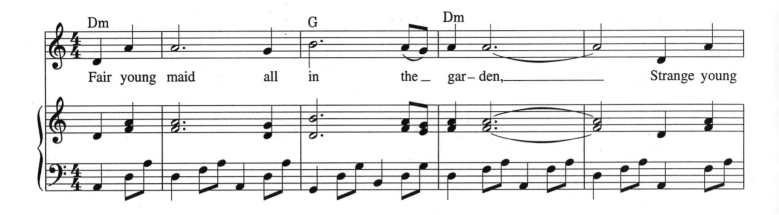

Fair young maid all in the gar–den,_____ Strange young

man pass her by._____ Said, "Fair

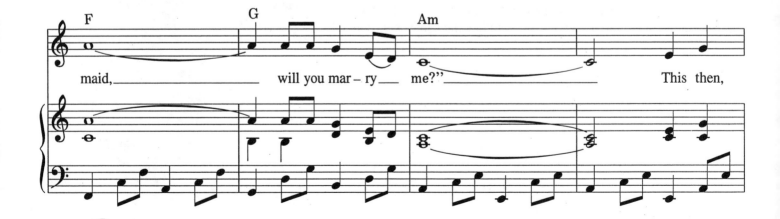

maid,_____ will you mar–ry me?"_____ This then,

sir, _____ was her re – ply. _____

"Oh no, kind sir, I cannot marry,
For I've a love who sails the sea.
He's been gone for these seven years,
Still no man shall marry me."

"What if he's in battle slain?
Or drowned in the deep salt sea?
What if he's found another love,
And that they both married be?"

"If he's in some battle slain,
I'll die when the moon doth wane.
If he's drowned in the deep salt sea,
I'll be true to his memory.

"If he's found another love,
And if they both married be,
Then I wish them happiness,
Where they dwell across the sea."

He picked her up all in his arms,
Kisses gave her, one, two, three.
"Weep no more, my own true love,
I'm your long-lost John Riley."

William Taylor

Wil – liam Tay – lor was a brisk young sail – or, He who court – ed a la – dy fair. Bells were ring – ing, sail – ors sing – ing, As to church they did re – pair.

Thirty couple at the wedding,
All were dressed in rich array.
'Stead of William being married,
He was pressed and sent away.

She dressed up in man's apparel,
Man's apparel she put on,
And she followed her true lover;
For to find him she is gone.

Then the Captain stepped up to her,
Asking her, "What brought you here?"
"I am come to seek my true love,
Whom I lately loved so dear."

If you've come to see your true love,
Tell me what his name may be.
"O, his name is William Taylor,
From the Irish ranks came he."

"You rise early tomorrow morning,
You rise at the break of day;
There you'll see your true love William,
Walking with a lady gay."

She rose early the very next morning,
She rose up at break of day.
There she saw her true love William
Walking with a lady gay.

Sword and pistol then she ordered
To be brought at her command;
And she shot her true love William,
With the bride at his right hand.

If young folks in Wells or London
Were served the same as she served he,
Then young girls would not be undone;
Very scarce young men would be!

The Fish in
the Sea

The Bonnie Ship, The Diamond

Early in the 19th century, the Greenland Sea was fished nearly clean. Whalermen from Peterhead were attracted by the newly found grounds at the entrance to the Davis Strait (between Greenland and Canada)—the so-called Southwest Fishery. This song probably dates from the late 1820s. In 1830, one of the worst disasters of British whaling occurred when a large part of the fleet, including the *Diamond,* the *Resolution,* and the *Eliza Swan,* were locked in the far-northern ice of Melville Bay, Greenland. Twenty fine ships and scores of bold whalermen were lost.

The *Dia-mond* is a ship, my lads, For the Da-vis Strait she's bound, And the
Thom-son gives the or - der to sail the o - cean wide, Where the

quay it is all gar - nish-ed with bon - nie las - ses 'round. Cap-tain
sun it nev - er sets, my lad, no dark - ness dims _ the

sky. So it's cheer up, my lads, Let your hearts nev-er fail, While the

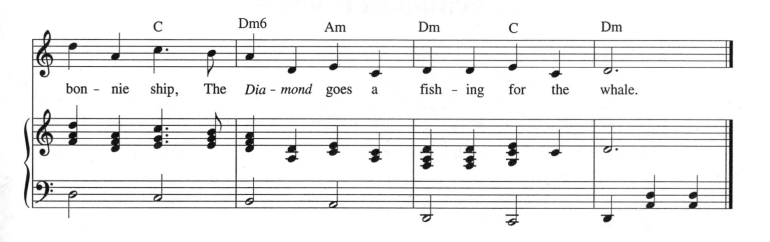

bon - nie ship, The *Dia - mond* goes a fish - ing for the whale.

Along the quay at Peterhead,
The lasses stand around,
Wi' their shawls all pulled about them
And the saut tears rinin' doon;
Don't you weep, my bonnie lass,
Though you be left behind,
For the rose will grow on Greenland's ice,
Before we change our mind. *Chorus*

Here's a health to the *Resolution,*
Likewise the *Eliza Swan,*
Here's a health to the *Battler of Montrose*
And the *Diamond,* ship of fame;
We wear the trousers of the white
And the jackets o' the blue,
When we return to Peterhead,
We'll ha'e sweethearts enoo. *Chorus*

It'll be bricht both day and nicht,
When the Greenland lads come hame,
Wi' a ship that's fu' o' oil, my lads,
And money to our name;
We'll make the cradles for to rock,
And the blankets for to tear.
And every lass in Peterhead sing
"Hushabye, my dear." *Chorus*

Greenland Fisheries

'Twas in eight – een hun – dred and fif – ty three, And of June the thir – teenth day, That our gal – lant ship her __ an – chor __ weighed, And for Green-land bore __ a – way, brave boys, And for Green – land bore __ a – way.

The look-out in the crosstree stood,
With a spy-glass in his hand,
"There's a whale, there's a whale, there's a whalefish," he cried,
"And she blows at every hand"....

The Captain stood on the quarter-deck,
And a fine little man was he,
"Overhaul! Overhaul! let your davit-tackles fall,
And launch your boats for sea"....

Now the boats were launched and the men aboard,
And the whale was in full view;
Resolv-ed was each seaman bold
To steer where the whalefish blew....

We struck that whale, the line paid out,
But she gave a flourish with her tail;
The boat capsized and four men were drowned,
And we never caught that whale....

"To lose the whale," our captain said,
"It grieves my heart full sore;
But oh! to lose four gallant men,
It grieves me ten times more"....

"The winter star doth now appear,
So, boys, we'll anchor weigh;
It's time to leave this cold country,
And homeward bear away"....

Oh, Greenland is a dreadful place,
A land that's never green,
Where there's ice and snow, and the whalefishes blow,
And the daylight's seldom seen....

89

Blow, Ye Winds, Westerly

Come all ye young sail – or – men, lis – ten to me,___ I'll sing you a

song of the fish of the sea. Then blow, ye winds, west – er – ly,

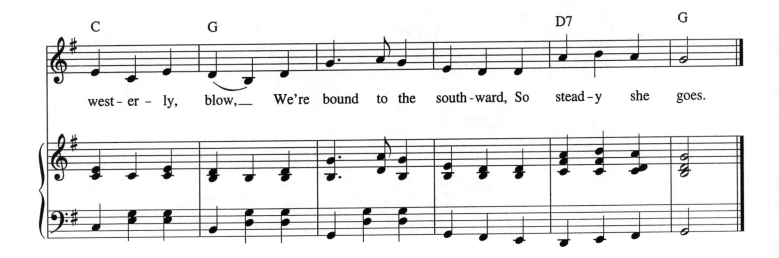

west – er – ly, blow,___ We're bound to the south – ward, So stead – y she goes.

Oh, first come the whale, the biggest of all,
He clumb up aloft and let every sail fall. *Chorus*

And next come the mackerel with his striped back,
He hauled aft the sheets and he boarded each tack. *Chorus*

Then come the porpoise with his short snout,
He went to the wheel, calling "Ready! About!" *Chorus*

Then come the smelt, the smallest of all,
He jumped to the poop and sung out, "Topsail, haul!" *Chorus*

The herring came saying, "I'm king of the seas,
If you want any wind I will blow you a breeze." *Chorus*

Next come the codfish with his chuckle-head,
He went to the main-chains to heave at the lead. *Chorus*

Last come the flounder, as flat as the ground,
Saying, "Damn your eyes, chuckle-head, mind how you sound!" *Chorus*

Boothbay Whale

step right up and take a lit-tle swig, And you'll soon see a Booth-bay whale.

Says Captain Pete, "I've harpooned tuna,
And caught them with my rig,
But I ain't gettin' near no eighty-foot whale,
That fish is too darned big."
Well, Skipper Jake was a ready man,
Though he had a wooden leg.
Says he, "I think I'll catch that whale;
Let me have the old rum keg." *Chorus*

Well, he stood on the bow of the *Nancy U.*,
And followed that whale for a ride,
And when that whale he surfaced and blowed,
He steered her to starboard side.
The whale blowed steam from his big spout hole,
While Jake took a slug from his keg;
And before he could dive, Jake jumped on his back,
Hangin' on with his one good leg. *Chorus*

Well, Jake took his keg and used it like a plug,
Pushed it tight in the old whale's spout.
He kicked it hard, then jumped on board
Sayin', "Boys, it will never come out."
Well, the whale he blew, he puffed, he heaved,
And the boys all gave a shout;
And the very next time he 'rose to blow,
He blew his brains right out. *Chorus*

You bold seafarin' whalermen,
You've wasted all these years,
With race boats, harpoons, ropes and hooks,
And all that other gear.
All you need is a big ol' plug,
Next time you see him spout,
Just kick it in, sit back and rest,
While he blows his brains right out. *Chorus*

If you ever meet a fisherman from Boothbay, Maine,
And you want to hear a dreadful tale,
Well, step right up and offer him a keg,
And learn how to catch a Boothbay whale. *Chorus*

Blow, Ye Winds, In The Morning

'Tis ad – ver – tised in Bos – ton, New York and Buf – fa – lo, Five

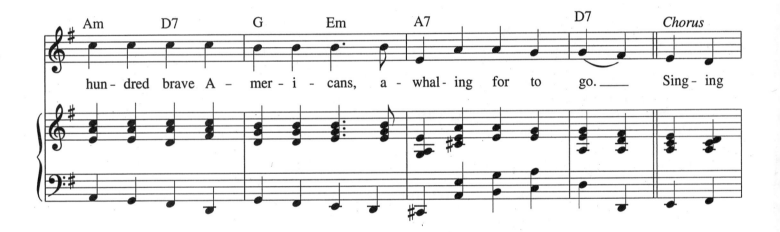

hun – dred brave A – mer – i – cans, a – whal – ing for to go. ____ Sing – ing

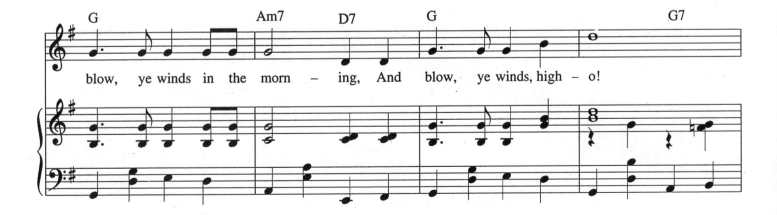

blow, ye winds in the morn – ing, And blow, ye winds, high – o!

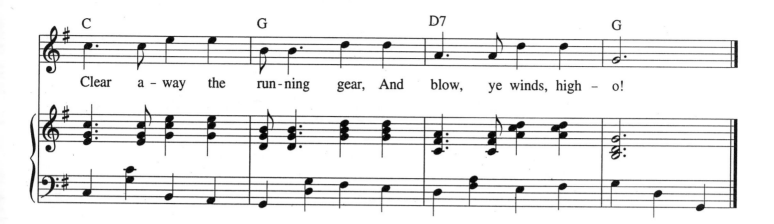

Clear a-way the run-ning gear, And blow, ye winds, high - o!

They send you to New Bedford,
That famous whaling port,
And give you to some land-sharks
To board and fit you out. *Chorus*

They send you to a boarding-house,
There for a time to dwell;
The thieves there they are thicker
Than the other side of hell! *Chorus*

They tell you of the clipper-ships,
A-going in and out,
And say you'll take five hundred sperm,
Before you're six months out. *Chorus*

It's now we're out to sea, my boys,
The wind begins to blow,
One half of the watch is sick on deck
And the other half below. *Chorus*

The skipper's on the quarter-deck
A-squinting at the sails,
When up aloft the look-out
Sights a school of whales. *Chorus*

Now clear away the boats, my boys,
And after him we'll travel,
But if you get too near his fluke,
He'll kick you to the devil! *Chorus*

Now we've got him turned up,
We tow him alongside,
We over with our blubber hooks
And rob him of his hide. *Chorus*

Next comes the stowing down, my boys,
'Twill take both night and day,
And you'll have fifty cents apiece
On the one hundred and ninetieth day. *Chorus*

Now we are bound into Tuckoona,
Full more in their power,
Where the skippers can buy the Consul up
For half a barrel of flour. *Chorus*

When we get home, our ship made fast,
And we get through our sailing,
A winding glass around we'll pass
And damn this blubber-whaling. *Chorus*

The Montaukers

Music and last verse
by Jerry Silverman

This chos-en re-treat was the home and the seat of the bold and ad-ven-tur-ous whal-er;_____ And for years had sup-plied to the world far and wide, the mo-del A-mer-i-can sail-or._____

For no maiden would look
On a young man who took
To a land life of torpor and
   stupor,
When the scene was here laid
Of the *Sea Lion's* raid
Of our national novelist, Cooper.

In these prosperous years
It had shipyards and piers
And coopers and riggers and caulkers,
Ship chandlers, sail makers,
And ship biscuit bakers,
And the whalemen then known as
   Montaukers.

Here's a health to them all
Who follow the call,
Who sail on the perilous waters.
Montaukers are sailors,
And bold, fearless whalers—
Watch out for your wives and your
   daughters!

We'll Rant And We'll Roar

Chorus:

We'll rant and we'll roar like true-born young whalermen,
We'll rant and we'll roar on deck and below,
Until we strike Gay Head on old Martha's Vineyard,
And straight up the channel to New Bedford we'll go.

I went to a dance one night in old Tumbez,
There were lots of fine girls there as nice as you'd wish,
There was one pretty maiden a-chewin' tobacco,
Just like a young kitten, a-chewin' fresh fish. *Chorus*

The Squid-Jiggin' Ground

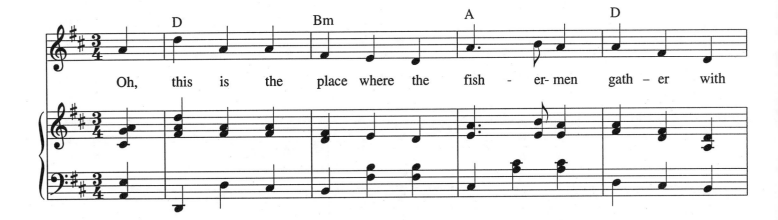

Oh, this is the place where the fish - er- men gath – er with

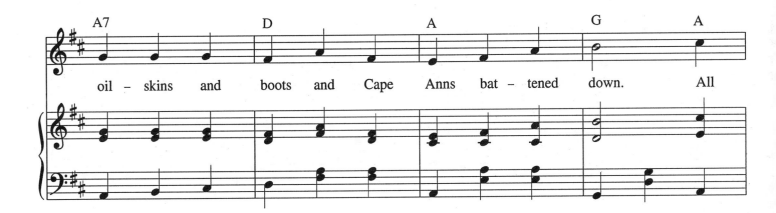

oil – skins and boots and Cape Anns bat – tened down. All

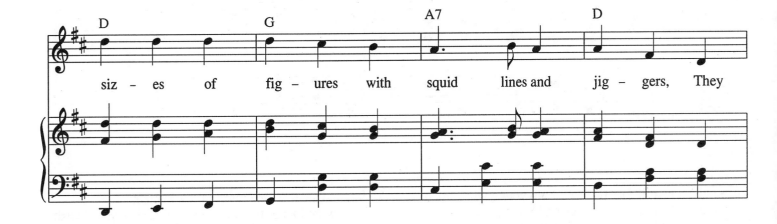

siz – es of fig – ures with squid lines and jig - gers, They

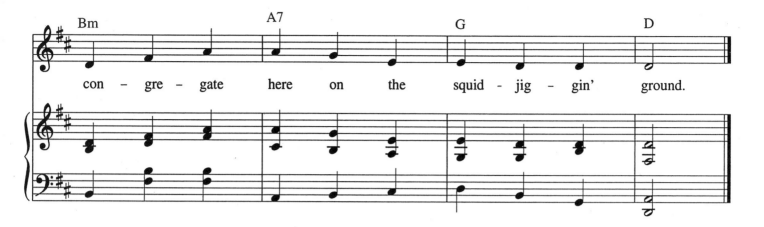

con - gre - gate here on the squid - jig - gin' ground.

Some are workin' their jiggers while others are yarnin',
There's some standin' up and there's more lyin' down;
While all kinds of fun, jokes and tricks are begun
As they wait for the squid on the squid-jiggin' ground.

There's men of all ages and boys in the bargain;
There's old Billy Cave and there's young Raymond Brown;
There's a red rantin' Tory out here in a dory,
A-runnin' down squids on the squid-jiggin' ground.

There's men from the Harbour and men from the Tickle,
In all kinds of motorboats, green, grey and brown;
Right yonder is Bobby and with him is Nobby,
He's chawin' hardtack on the squid-jiggin' ground.

God bless my sou'wester, there's Skipper John Chaffey;
He's the best hand at squid-jiggin' here, I'll be bound.
Hello! What's the row? Why, he's jiggin' one now,
The very first squid on the squid-jiggin' ground.

The man with the whiskers is old Jacob Steele;
He's gettin' well up but he's still pretty sound;
While Uncle Bob Hawkins wears six pairs of stockin's
Whenever he's out on the squid-jiggin' ground.

Holy smoke! What a scuffle! All hands are excited.
'Tis a wonder to me that there's nobody drowned.
There's a bustle, confusion, a wonderful hustle,
They're all jiggin' squids on the squid-jiggin' ground.

Says Bobby, "The squids are on top of the water,
I just got me jigger 'bout one fathom down,"
When a squid in the boat squirted right down his throat,
And he's swearin' like mad on the squid-jiggin' ground.

There's poor Uncle Billy, his whiskers are spattered
With spots of the squid juice that's flying around;
One poor little b'y got it right in the eye,
But they don't give a darn on the squid-jiggin' ground.

Now if ever you feel inclined to go squiddin',
Leave your white shirts and collars behind in the town,
And if you get cranky without yer silk hanky,
You'd better steer clear of the squid-jiggin' ground.

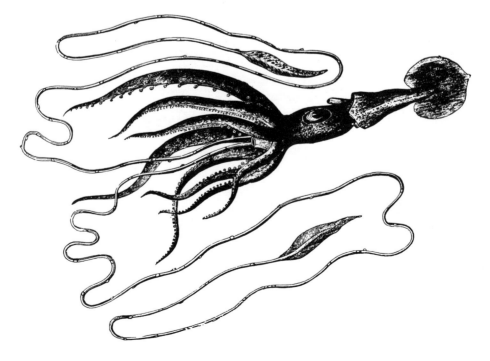

99

Haul Away Together

Cheer'ly Man

Solo

E   B7   **Crew**   E

Oh, Sal - ly Rack - et, Hi - oh! _____ Cheer - 'ly, man!

Solo

F#m   B7   **Crew**   E

Pawned my best jack - et, Hi - oh! _____ Cheer - 'ly, man!

Solo

E   **Crew**   A

And sold the tick - et, Hi - oh! Cheer - 'ly, man!

Solo

E   B7   **Crew**   E

Oh, Haul - ee, hi - oh, _____ Cheer - 'ly, man!

Oh, Nancy Dawson, Hi-oh!...	Oh, Betsey Baker, Hi-oh!...	Oh, Kitty Carson, Hi-oh!...	Avast there, avast, Hi-oh!...
She's got a notion, Hi-oh!...	Lived in Long Acre, Hi-oh!...	Jilted the parson, Hi-oh!...	Make the fall fast, Hi-oh!...
For our old bo'sun, Hi-oh!....	Married a Quaker, Hi-oh!....	Married a mason, Hi-oh!....	Make it well fast, Hi-oh!....

102

So Handy

Oh, up a-loft this yard __ must go, So han-dy, my boys, so han-dy! __ Oh, up __ a-loft from down be-low, So han-dy, my boys, so han dy! __

We'll hoist it high before we go...
And when it's up we'll leave it so....

Oh, sing and haul and haul and sing...
Right up aloft this yard we'll bring....

Stretch her leach and show her clew...
A few more pulls to bring her through....

I thought I heard the first mate say...
"Give one more pull and then belay"....

A Long Time Ago

A - way down South where I ___ was born, To me way hay ___ i - oh, A-

mong the fields ___ of gold - en corn, A long time ___ a - go. ___

I made up my mind to go to sea...
I made up my mind to go to sea....

I wish to God I'd never been born...
To go rambling round and round Cape Horn....

Around Cape Horn with frozen sails...
Around Cape Horn to fish for whales....

Around Cape Horn where wild winds blow...
Around Cape Horn through sleet and snow....

Around Cape Horn we've got to go...
Around Cape Horn to Callao....

Poor Old Man

I say, old man, your horse will die, And I say so, and I
know so. I say, old man, your horse will die, Oh, poor old man.

And if he dies we'll tan his skin...   (2)

And if he lives we'll ride him agin!...   (2)

We'll hoist him at the main yardarm...   (2)

And now he's dead we'll bury him deep...   (2)

Blood-Red Roses

You've had your advance and to sea you must go...
A-chasin' whales through the frost and the snow.... *Chorus*

Oh, my old mother, she wrote to me...
My dearest son, come home from the sea.... *Chorus*

But 'round Cape Horn you've got to go...
For that is where them whalefish blow.... *Chorus*

Just one more and that'll do...
For we're the gang to kick her through.... *Chorus*

Haul Away, Joe

"The shantyman with originality and a reputation to maintain tried not to repeat the same line twice. If his story came to an end before the job was over, he fell back on a series of lines describing the piece of work under way, drawn from a common stock used for 'piecing out' on such occasions." (Joanna Colcord, *Songs of American Sailormen*)

Way, haul a-way, we'll haul a-way to-geth – er,____ Way, haul a-way, we'll haul a-way, Joe.

Way, haul a-way, we'll haul for bet – ter weath – er, ____ Way, haul a-way, we'll haul a-way, Joe.

Now when I was a little lad, me mother always told me...
That if I didn't kiss the girls, me lips would all go mouldy.... *Chorus*

King Louis was the king of France before the Revolution...
King Louis got his head cut off and spiled his constitution.... *Chorus*

Once I had a scolding wife, she wasn't very civil...
I clapped a plaster on her mouth and sent her to the divil.... *Chorus*

Way, haul away, we'll haul for better weather...
Way, haul away, we'll haul and hang together.... *Chorus*

107

Haul On The Bowline

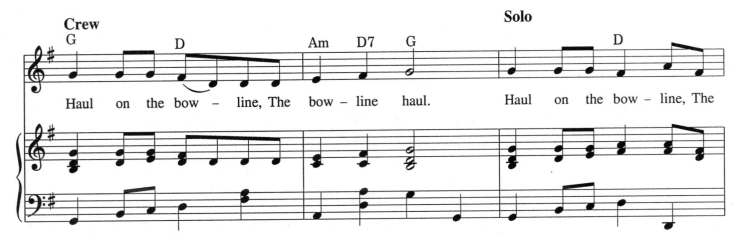

Haul on the bowline, Kitty is my darling...
Haul on the bowline, Kitty lives at Liverpool....

Haul on the bowline, the old man is a-growlin'...
Haul on the bowline, it's a far cry to payday....

Haul on the bowline, so early in the mornin'...
Haul on the bowline, I give you all fair warnin'....

The Black Ball Line

I served my time on the Black Ball Line, To me way, aye, aye, hur -

rah. ____ In the Black Ball Line I served my time, Hur - rah for the Black Ball Line.

The Black Ball ships they are good and true...
And they are the ships for me and you....

For once there was a Black Ball ship...
That fourteen knots an hour could clip....

You will surely find a rich gold mine...
Just take a trip in the Black Ball line....

Just take a trip to Liverpool...
To Liverpool, that Yankee school....

The Yankee sailors you'll see there...
With red-top boots and short-cut hair....

Hieland Laddie

Was you ever in Quebec?__ Bonnie laddie, hieland laddie,
Stowing timber on the deck,__ My bonnie hieland laddie.

Chorus

Hey ho, and away we go, Bonnie laddie, hieland laddie.
Hey ho, away we go, My bonnie hieland laddie.

Was you ever in Callao...
Where the girls are never slow.... *Chorus*

Was you ever in Baltimore...
Dancing on that sanded floor.... *Chorus*

Was you on the Brummalow...
Where Yankee boys are all the go.... *Chorus*

Was you ever in Dundee...
There some pretty ships you'll see.... *Chorus*

Lowlands

O was you ev – er in Mo - bile Bay? Low – lands,
low - lands,___ A - way,_____ my John, A –
screw - in' cot – ton___ by the day. My dol- lar and a half a day.

The white man's pay is rather high...
The black man's pay is rather low....

O my old mother, she wrote to me...
She wrote to me to come home from sea....

The Bullgine Run

It Was Sad When That Great Ship Went Down

The Bold Fisherman

There was a bold fish-er-man who sailed out from Pim-be-co to

slew the wild cod-fish and the bold mack-er-al. When he ar-rived off

Pim-be-co, the storm-y winds did wild-ly blow, His lit-tle boat went

wib-ble wob-ble, and o-ver-board sprang he. "Twink-i doo-dle dum, twin-ki

doo-dle dum," 'Twas the high-ly in-ter-est-ing song he sung. "Twin-ki doo-dle dum, twin-ki doo-dle dum," sang the bold fish-er-man.

He wriggled and scriggled in the water, so briny-o,
He yellowed and bellowed for help but in vain.
Then downward he did gently glide
To the bottom of the silvery tide;
But previously to this he cried,
"Fare thee well, Mar-i-Jane!" *Chorus*

His ghost walked at midnight to the bedside of his Mar-i-Jane.
He told her how dead he was; said she, "I'll go mad.
Since my lovey is so dead," said she,
"All joy on earth has fled for me;
I never more will happy be."
And she went staring mad. *Chorus*

The Titanic

On the night of April 14–15, 1912, the "unsinkable" ocean liner *Titanic* struck an iceberg off the Grand Banks of Newfoundland on her maiden voyage and sank with a loss of 1,513 lives. The disaster shocked the astounded the world. This song, however, is generally sung in a rousing, almost good-natured manner.

Oh, they built the ship Ti - tan - ic to sail the o - cean blue, And they

thought they had a ship that the wa - ter would nev - er go through; But the

Lord's al - migh - ty hand said that ship would nev - er land, It was

sad when that great ship went down. It was sad, it was sad, It was sad when that great ship went down.

(to the bot-tom of the)

Hus-bands and wives, lit-tle chil-dren lost their lives. It was sad when that great ship went down.

Oh, they sailed from England's shore
'Bout a thousand miles or more,
When the rich refused to associate with the poor,
So they put them down below,
Where they'd be the first to go,
It was sad when that great ship went down. *Chorus*

Oh, the boat was full of sin,
And the sides about to burst,
When the captain shouted, "Women and children first!"
Oh, the captain tried to wire,
But the lines were all on fire,
It was sad when that great ship went down. *Chorus*

Oh, they swung the lifeboats out
O'er the deep and raging sea,
And the band struck up with "A-Nearer, My God, to Thee."
Little children wept and cried,
As the waves swept o'er the side,
It was sad when that great ship went down. *Chorus*

The Ship That Never Returned

On a sum - mer's day, while the waves were rip - pling, With a
sweet fare - wells, while there were lov — ing sig - nals, While a

qui - et and a gen - tle breeze, A_____ ship set sail with a
form__ was__ yet dis - cerned; Though they knew it not, 'twas a

car - go la - den For a post be - yond the sea. There were
sol - emn part-ing, For the ship she nev - er re -

2. turned. *Chorus* Did she ev - er re - turn? No, she nev - er re - turned, And her

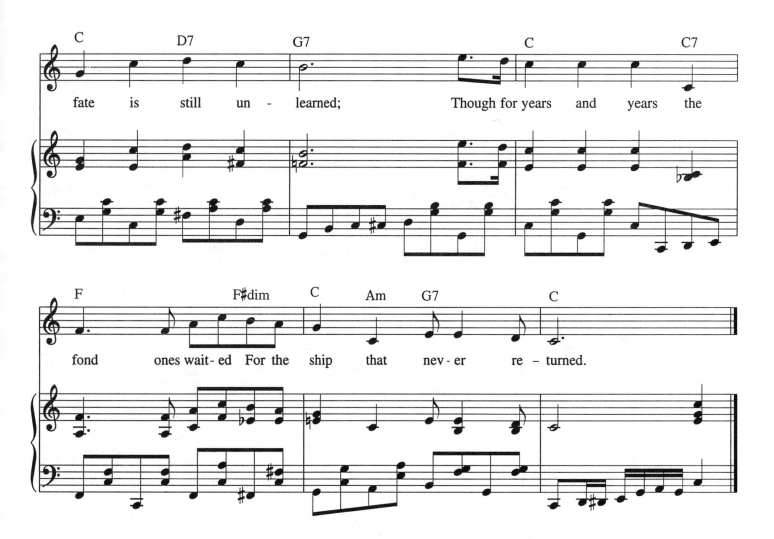

fate is still un - learned; Though for years and years the

fond ones wait- ed For the ship that nev- er re - turned.

Said a feeble lad to his anxious mother,
"I must cross the wide, wide sea;
For they say, perchance, in a foreign climate,
There is health and strength for me."
'Twas a gleam of hope in a maze of danger,
And her heart for her youngest yearned;
Yet she sent him forth with a smile and blessing
On the ship that never returned. *Chorus*

"Only one more trip," said a gallant seaman,
As he kissed his weeping wife;
"Only one more bag of the golden treasure,
And 'twill last us all through life.
Then I'll spend my days in my cozy cottage,
And enjoy the rest I've earned";
But alas! poor man! for he sailed commander
Of the ship that never returned. *Chorus*

Deep Blue Sea

Deep blue sea, ba-by, deep blue sea. Deep blue
sea, ba-by, deep blue sea. Deep blue sea, ba-by, deep blue
sea. It was Wil-lie what got drown-ded in the deep blue sea.

Dig his grave with a silver spade,   (3)
It was Willie what got drownded in the deep blue sea. *Chorus*

Golden sun bring him back again,   (3)
It was Willie what got drownded in the deep blue sea. *Chorus*

Lower him down with a golden chain,   (3)
It was Willie what got drownded in the deep blue sea. *Chorus*

Run Come See Jerusalem

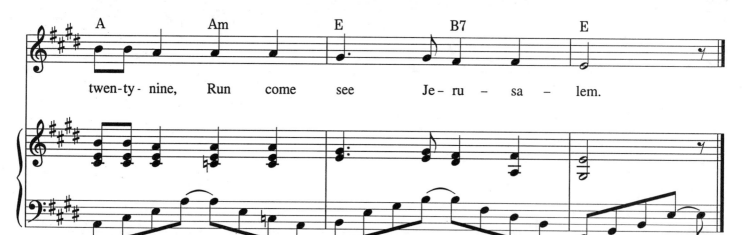

That day they were talking 'bout a storm in the islands... (2)	Right then it was a big sea built up in the northwest... (2)
That day there were three ships leaving out the harbor... (2)	My God, when the first wave hit the *Pretoria*... (2)
It was the *Ethel,* the *Myrtle* and the *Pretoria*... (2)	My God, there were thirty-three souls on the water... (2)
They were bound for the island of Andros... (2)	My God, now George Brown he was the captain... (2)
The *Pretoria* was out on the ocean... (2)	He said, "Come now, witness your judgment"... (2)

There'll be no more waiting on Andros... (2)

The Golden Vanity

In hundreds of variations, this ballad has long been one of the most popular on both sides of the Atlantic. Francis J. Child traces the song back to a 17th-century broadside in which Sir Walter Raleigh is named as the owner of the ship (there named *The Sweet Trinity*).

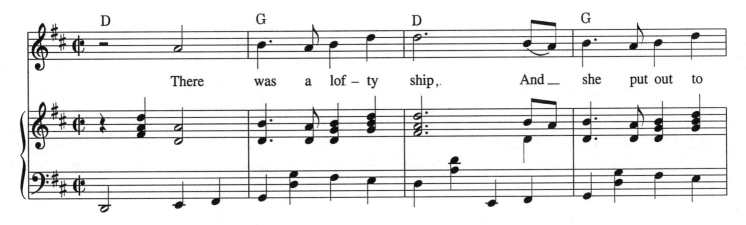

There was a lof – ty ship, And — she put out to

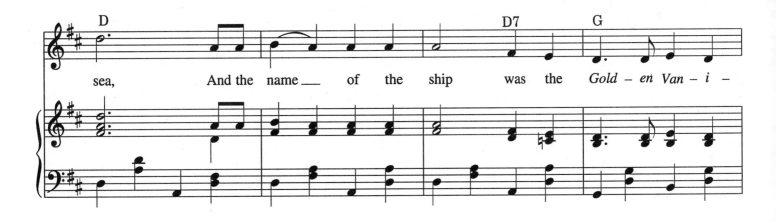

sea, And the name — of the ship was the *Gold – en Van – i –*

ty. As she sailed up-on the low _____ and — lone – some

low, _____ As she sailed up-on the lone — some _ sea. _____

She had not been out but two weeks or three,
When she was overtaken by a *Turkish Revelee,*
As she sailed upon....

Then up spake our little cabin boy,
Saying, "What will you give me if I will them destroy,
If I sink them in...."

"O, the man that them destroys," our captain then replied,
"Five thousand pounds and my daughter for his bride,
If he sinks them in...."

Then the boy smote his breast and down jumped he,
He swum until he came to the *Turkish Revelee,*
As she sailed upon....

He had a little tool that was made for the use,
He bored nine holes in her hull at once,
And he sunk her in....

He swum back to his ship and he beat upon the side,
Cried, "Captain, pick me up for I'm wearied with the tide,
I am sinking in...."

"No! I will not pick you up," the captain then replied,
"I will shoot you, I will drown you, I will sink you in the tide.
I will sink you in...."

"If it was not for the love that I bear for your men,
I would do unto you as I did unto them,
I would sink you in...."

Then the boy bowed his head and down sunk he;
Farewell, farewell to the *Golden Vanity,*
As she sails upon....

123

The Mermaid

'Twas Fri – day __ morn when we __ set __ sail, And we were not far from the land, When our cap – tain __ spied a love-ly mer – maid with a comb and a glass in her hand.

Chorus Oh, the o – cean waves may roll, And the storm – y seas may blow, While __

we poor — sail-ors go skip-ping to the top, And the land – lub-bers lie down be –

low, be-low, be-low, And the land – lub-bers lie down be – low.

Then up spake the captain of our gallant ship,
And a well-spoken man was he.
"I have me a wife in Salem town,
And tonight she a widow will be." *Chorus*

Then up spake the cook of our gallant ship,
And a well-spoken cook was he.
"I care much more for my kettles and my pots
Than I do for the bottom of the sea." *Chorus*

Then up spake the cabin boy of our gallant ship,
And a well-spoken youth was he.
"There's nary a soul in Salem town
Who cares a bit for me." *Chorus*

Then three times around went our gallant ship,
And three times around went she.
Then three times around went our gallant ship,
And she sank to the bottom of the sea. *Chorus*

Murder on the
High Seas

The Flying Cloud

The "Guinea trade"—slaving—openly carried on by American ships in the 18th century, was prohibited by several Acts of Congress between 1807 and 1823. This song probably dates from somewhere between 1819 and 1825, when the West Indies were finally cleared of pirates by combined United States and European naval powers. Before this date the Caribbean was infested by slavers turned pirates and pirates turned slavers as the winds changed.

My name is Ed – ward Hol – lan – der, as you may un – der – stand, I was

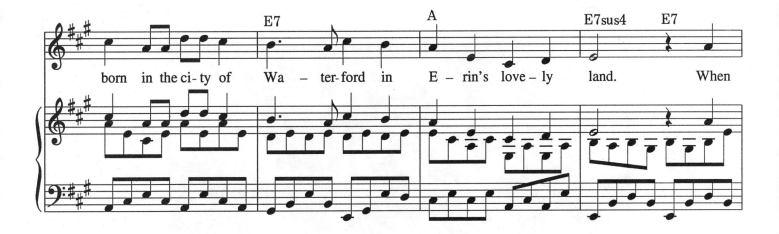

born in the ci – ty of Wa – ter-ford in E – rin's love – ly land. When

I was young and in my prime, fair for – tune on me smiled; My

pa – rents reared me ten – der – ly, I was their on – ly child.

My father bound me to a trade in Waterford's fair town,
He bound me to a cooper there, by the name of William Brown.
I served my master faithfully for eighteen months or more,
Till I shipped on board of the *Ocean Queen,* belonging to Tramore.

When we came unto Bermuda's isle, there I met with Captain Moore,
The commander of the *Flying Cloud,* hailing from Baltimore,
He asked me if I'd ship with him, on a slaving voyage to go,
To the burning shores of Africa, where the sugar cane does grow.

It was after some weeks' sailing we arrived off Africa's shore,
And five hundred of these poor slaves, my boys, from their native land we bore.
We made them walk in on a plank, and we stowed them down below;
Scarce eighteen inches to a man was all they had to go.

The plague and fever came on board, swept half of them away;
We dragged their bodies up on deck and hove them in the sea.
It was better for the rest of them if they had died before,
Than to work under brutes of planters in Cuba for ever more.

It was after stormy weather we arrived off Cuba's shore,
And we sold them to the planters there, to be slaves for ever more.
For the rice and the coffee seed to sow beneath the broiling sun,
There to lead a wretched, lonely life till their career was run.

It's now our money is all spent, we must go to sea again,
When Captain Moore he came on deck and said unto us men,
"There is gold and silver to be had if with me you'll remain,
And we'll hoist the pirate flag aloft, and we'll scour the Spanish Main."

We all agreed but three young men who told us them to land,
And two of them was Boston boys, the other from Newfoundland.
I wish to God I'd joined those men and went with them on shore,
Than to lead a wild and reckless life, serving under Captain Moore.

The *Flying Cloud* was a Yankee ship of five hundred tons or more;
She could outsail any clipper ship hailing out of Baltimore.
With her canvas white as the driven snow, and on it there's no specks,
And forty men and fourteen guns she carried on her decks.

It's oft I've seen that gallant ship, with the wind abaft her beam,
With her royals and her stunsails set, a sight for to be seen,
With the curling wave from her slipper bow, a sailor's joy to feel,
And the canvas taut in the whistling breeze, logging fourteen off the reel.

We sank and plundered many a ship down on the Spanish Main,
Caused many a wife and orphan in sorrow to remain;
To them we gave no quarter, but gave them watery graves,
For the saying of our captain was that dead men tell no tales.

Pursued we were by many a ship, by frigates and liners too,
Till at last a British man-o'-war, the *Dunmore,* hove in view.
She fired a shot across our bow, as we sailed before the wind,
Then a chainshot cut our mainmast down, and we fell far behind.

Our crew they beat to quarters as she ranged up alongside,
And soon across our quarter-deck there ran a crimson tide.
We fought till Captain Moore was killed and twenty of our men,
Till a bombshell set our ship on fire, we had to surrender then.

It's next to Newgate we were brought, bound down in iron chains,
For the sinking and the plundering of ships on the Spanish Main.
The judge he found us guilty, we were condemned to die;
Young men, a warning by me take, and shun all piracy.

Then fare you well, old Waterford, and the girl that I adore;
I'll never kiss your cheek again, or squeeze your hand no more.
For whisky and bad company first made a wretch of me;
Young men, a warning by me take, and shun all piracy.

Captain Kidd

William Kidd (*c.* 1645–1701) received a king's commission in 1696 to arrest and bring to trial all pirates. He sailed from Plymouth in May 1696 for New York, where he filled up his crew, and in 1697 reached Madagascar, the pirates' principal rendezvous. He made no effort whatsoever to hunt them down. On the contrary, he associated himself with a notorious pirate named Culliford. During 1698–1699, complaints reached the British government as to the character of his proceedings. He sailed again for America and buried some of his treasure on Gardiner's Island (off the east end of Long Island). He was arrested in Boston in July 1699 and was sent to England, where he was tried, convicted, and executed.

Oh! my parents taught me well, as I sailed, as I sailed,
Oh, my parents taught me well, as I sailed.
My parents taught me well, to shun the gates of hell,
But against them I rebelled, as I sailed, as I sailed,
But against them I rebelled, as I sailed.

I murdered William Moore, as I sailed, as I sailed,
I murdered William Moore, as I sailed.
I murdered William Moore and left him in his gore,
Not many leagues from shore, as I sailed, as I sailed,
Not many leagues from shore, as I sailed.

And being cruel still, as I sailed, as I sailed,
And being cruel still, as I sailed,
And being cruel still, my gunner I did kill,
And his precious blood did spill, as I sailed, as I sailed,
And his precious blood did spill, as I sailed.

My mate was sick and died, as I sailed, as I sailed,
My mate was sick and died, as I sailed.
My mate was sick and died, which me much terrified.
He called me to his bedside, as I sailed, as I sailed,
He called me to his bedside, as I sailed.

And unto me did say, "See me die, see me die,"
And unto me did say, "See me die."
And unto me did say, "Take warning now by me,
There comes a reckoning day, you must die, you must die,
There comes a reckoning day, you must die."

I steered from sound to sound, as I sailed, as I sailed,
I steered from sound to sound, as I sailed.
I steered from sound to sound, and many ships I found,
And most of them I drowned, as I sailed, as I sailed,
And most of them I drowned, as I sailed.

I spied three ships from Spain, as I sailed, as I sailed,
I spied three ships from Spain, as I sailed.
I spied three ships from Spain, I fired on them amain
Till most of them were slain, as I sailed, as I sailed,
Till most of them were slain, as I sailed.

I'd ninety bars of gold, as I sailed, as I sailed,
I'd ninety bars of gold, as I sailed.
I'd ninety bars of gold, and dollars manifold.
With riches uncontrolled, as I sailed, as I sailed,
With riches uncontrolled, as I sailed.

Then fourteen ships I saw, as I sailed, as I sailed,
Then fourteen ships I saw, as I sailed.
Then fourteen ships I saw, and brave men they were.
Ah! they were too much for me, as I sailed, as I sailed,
Ah! they were too much for me, as I sailed.

To Newgate I am cast, and must die, and must die,
To Newgate I am cast, and must die.
To Newgate I am cast, with sad and heavy heart,
To receive my just desert, I must die, I must die,
To receive my just desert, I must die.

Take warning now by me, for I must die, I must die,
Take warning now by me, for I must die.
Take warning now by me, and shun bad company,
Lest you come to hell with me, for I must die, I must die,
Lest you come to hell with me, for I must die.

High Barbary

The coastal population of northern Africa has in past ages been addicted to piratical attacks on shores and shipping of Europe opposite. The conquest of Granada by the Catholic sovereigns of Spain drove many Moors into exile. They revenged themselves by piratical attacks on the Spanish coast. The first half of the 17th century may be described as the flowering time of the Barbary pirates. More than 20,000 captives were said to be imprisoned in Algiers alone. In 1655 the British admiral Robert Blake was sent out on a major punitive expedition. A long series of similar expeditions was undertaken by the British fleet during the reign of Charles II. In the 1680s the French bombarded Algiers, but the piracy continued into the 19th century. The "Marines' Hymn" ("From the halls of Montezuma to the shores of Tripoli...") commemorates American involvement in 1801–05 and again in 1815. In 1824 another British fleet under Admiral Sir Harry Neal had again to bombard Algiers. The great pirate city was not in fact thoroughly tamed until its conquest by France in 1830.

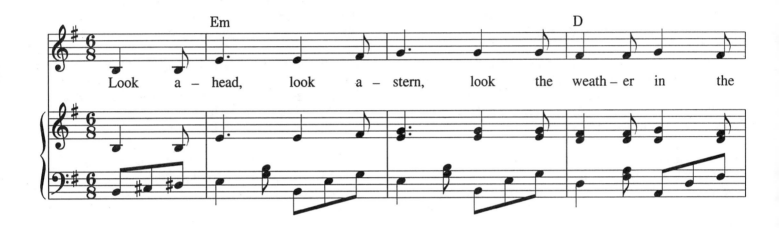

Look a – head, look a – stern, look the weath – er in the

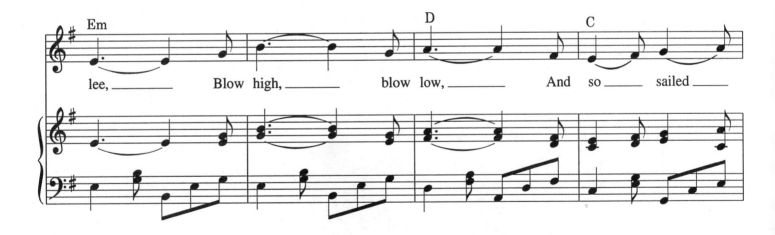

lee, _____ Blow high, _____ blow low, _____ And so _____ sailed _____

we. There's a loft – y ship to star – board and she's sail – ing fast and

free, Sail — ing down a — long the coasts of High Bar — ba — ry.

"Oh, are you a pirate or a man-o'-war?" cried we....
"Oh, no I'm not a pirate but a man-o'-war," cried he....

"Then back up your topsails and heave your vessel to"....
"For we have got some letters to be carried home by you"....

"We'll back up our topsail and heave our vessel to"...
"But only in some harbor and along the side of you"....

For broadside and broadside they fought all on the main...
Until at last the frigate shot the pirate's mast away....

For quarter, for quarter, the saucy pirates cried...
But the quarter that we showed them was to sink them in the tide....

With cutlass and gun, oh, we fought for hours three...
The ship it was their coffin, and their grave it was the sea....

Henry Martin

In some versions of this pirate ballad, Henry Martin (or Andrew Bartin) defeats and taunts Captain Charles Stewart, officer of King George III. In others, it is Henry who is captured and hauled off to the gallows in England.

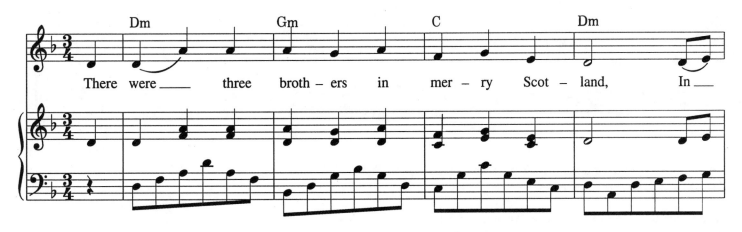

There were ___ three broth – ers in mer – ry Scot – land, In ___

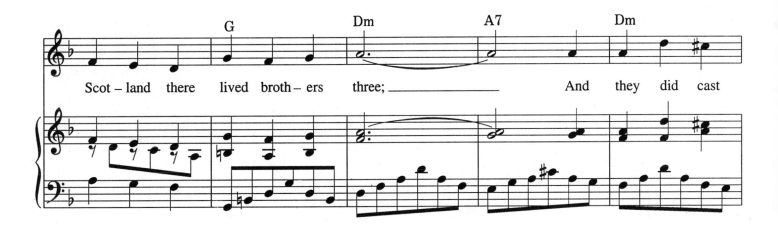

Scot – land there lived broth – ers three; ___ And they did cast

lots ___ which of them should go, ___ should go, ___ Should go, ___

For to turn rob–ber all on the salt sea.

The lot it fell upon Henry Martin,
The youngest of all three,
That he should turn robber all on the salt sea, salt sea, salt sea,
For to maintain his two brothers and he.

He had not been sailing but a long winter's night,
And part of a short winter's day,
When he espi-ed a lofty stout ship, stout ship, stout ship,
Come a-bibbing down on him straightway.

"Hello, hello," cried Henry Martin,
"What makes you sail so nigh?"
"I'm a rich merchant ship bound for fair London Town, London Town,
 London Town,
Will you please for to let me pass by?"

"Oh no, oh no," cried Henry Martin,
"That thing it never can be,
For I have turned robber all on the salt sea, salt sea, salt sea,
For to maintain my two brothers and me."

With broadside and broadside and at it they went
For fully two hours or three,
Till Henry Martin gave to her the death shot, the death shot, the death shot,
Heavily listing to starboard went she.

The rich merchant vessel was wounded full sore,
And straight to the bottom went she,
And Henry Martin sailed away on the sea, salt sea, salt sea,
For to maintain his two brothers and he.

Bad news, bad news to old England came,
Bad news to fair London Town,
There was a rich vessel and she's cast away,
And all of her merry men drowned.

. . . Rivers . . .

Boatman Dance

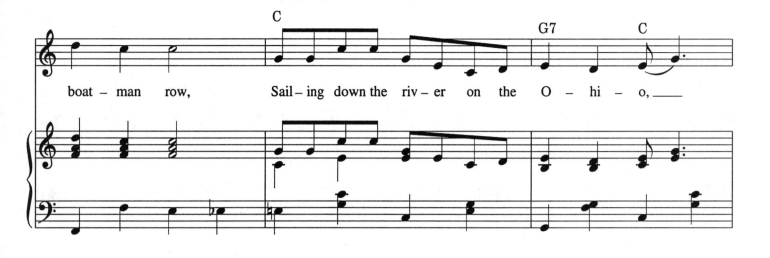

boat – man row, Sail – ing down the riv – er on the O – hi – o, ___

Heigh – ho, boat – man row, Sail – ing down the riv – er on the O – hi – o.

When the boatman gets on shore,
He spends his money and he works for more. *Chorus*

Never saw a pretty girl in my life,
But that she was a boatman's wife. *Chorus*

When the boatman blows his horn,
Look out, old man, your daughter is gone. *Chorus*

Sky-blue jacket and a tarpaulin hat,
Look out, boys, for the nine-tail cat. *Chorus*

The Lovely Ohio

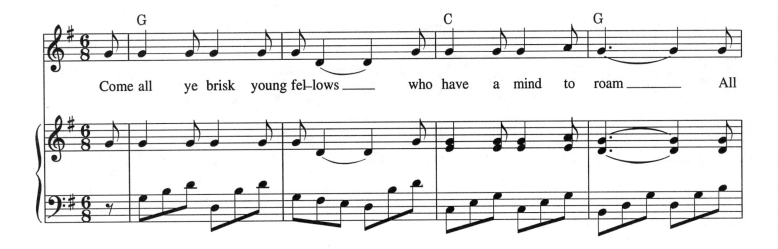

Come all ye brisk young fel-lows ___ who have a mind to roam ___ All

in some for — eign coun — ter—ee, a — long way from home; ___ All

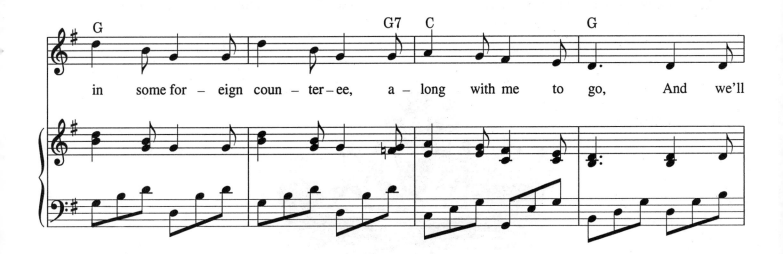

in some for — eign coun — ter—ee, a — long with me to go, And we'll

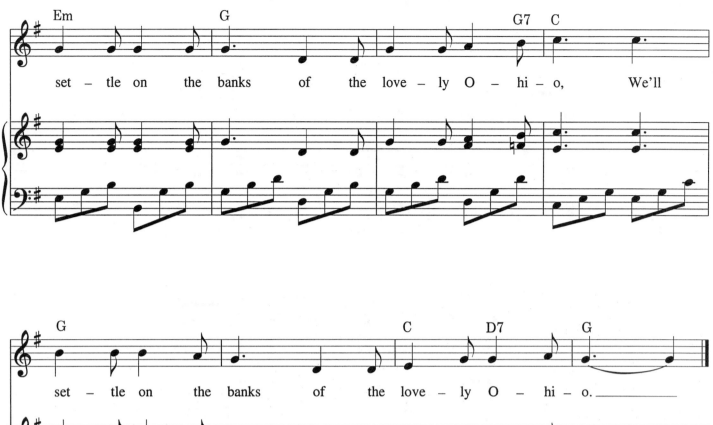

set – tle on the banks of the love – ly O – hi – o, We'll

set – tle on the banks of the love – ly O – hi – o. _____

Come all you pretty fair maids, spin us some yarn
To make us some nice clothing to keep ourselves warm.
For you can knit and sew, my loves, while we do reap and mow,
When we settle on the banks of the lovely Ohio. (2)

There are fishes in the river, just fitted for our use.
There's tall and lofty sugarcane that will give to us its juice,
There's every kind of game, my boys, also the buck and doe,
When we settle on the banks of the lovely Ohio. (2)

N.Y. Public Library Picture Collection

Cripple Creek

Girls on the Cripple Creek 'bout half grown,
Jump on a boy like a dog on a bone.
Roll my britches up to my knees,
I'll wade old Cripple Creek when I please. *Chorus*

Cripple Creek's wide and Cripple Creek's deep,
I'll wade old Cripple Creek afore I sleep,
Roads are rocky and the hillside's muddy,
And I'm so drunk that I can't stand steady. *Chorus*

Shenandoah

Oh, Shen – an – doah, _____ I long to hear you, A –

way, _____ You roll – ing riv – er, _____ Oh,

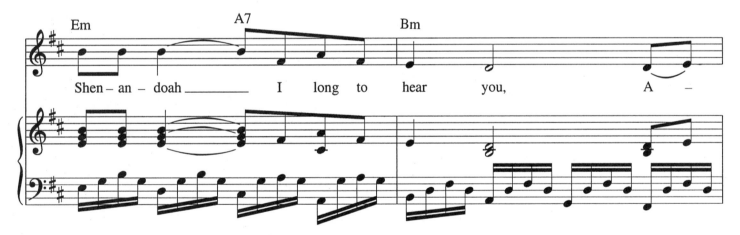

Shen – an – doah _____ I long to hear you, A –

way, _____ we're bound a – way _____ 'cross the

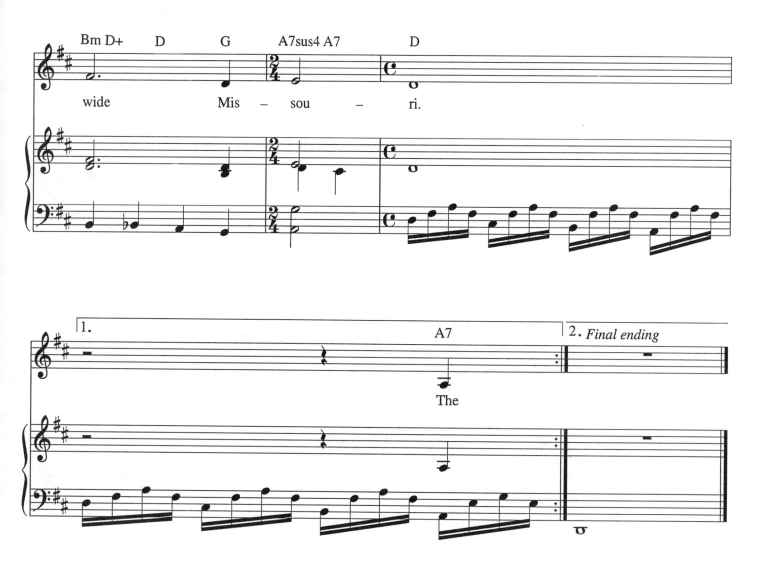

wide   Mis — sou — ri.

The

The white man loved the Indian maiden,
    Away, you rolling river,
With notions his canoe was laden. *Chorus*

O, Shenandoah, I love your daughter,
    Away, you rolling river,
I'll take her 'cross the rolling water. *Chorus*

O, Shenandoah, I'm bound to leave you,
    Away, you rolling river,
O, Shenandoah, I'll not deceive you. *Chorus*

N.Y. Public Library Picture Collection

The Memphis Blues

In 1909, W. C. Handy's band was hired to boost the campaign of Edward H. Crump, who was running for mayor of Memphis. Handy dusted off an anti-Crump song, which soon became the hit tune of the election. Crump was elected and eventually got a boulevard leading to the Mississippi River named after him.

By W. C. Handy

be my man,__ your ba-by's gon-na shake this town._____ Mis-ter
(gal), __

Crump don't 'low__ no eas-y ri – ders here,_____
Crump don't 'low__ it ain't goin' have_ it here,_____

Crump don't 'low – no eas-y ri – ders here. _____
Crump don't 'low – it ain't goin' have__ it here. _____

We don't care__ what Mis-ter Crump dont 'low, __ We gon – na bar'l- house an-y how, __ Mis-ter

1.
Crump don't 'low__ no eas—y ri – ders here._____ Mis-ter
Crump can go__ and catch his- self__ some

2.
air. _____

I'm go– in' down the riv- er go- in'
Mis – sis -sip- pi Riv- er,

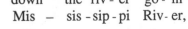

down to the riv – er, goin'to take my rock- in' chair, __ Goin' to the ri – ver, __
Mis – sis sip – pi Riv-er so ____ deep and wide, __ I said the Mis-sis – sip-pi

goin' to take my rock- in' chair, _____ Blues o- ver-take _ me,
Riv- er so _ deep and wide, _____ Man _ I love ____
(Gal)

goin to rock a- way from there. _____ Oh, the side
he is on the oth- er
(she)

Song Of The Volga Boatman

Russia

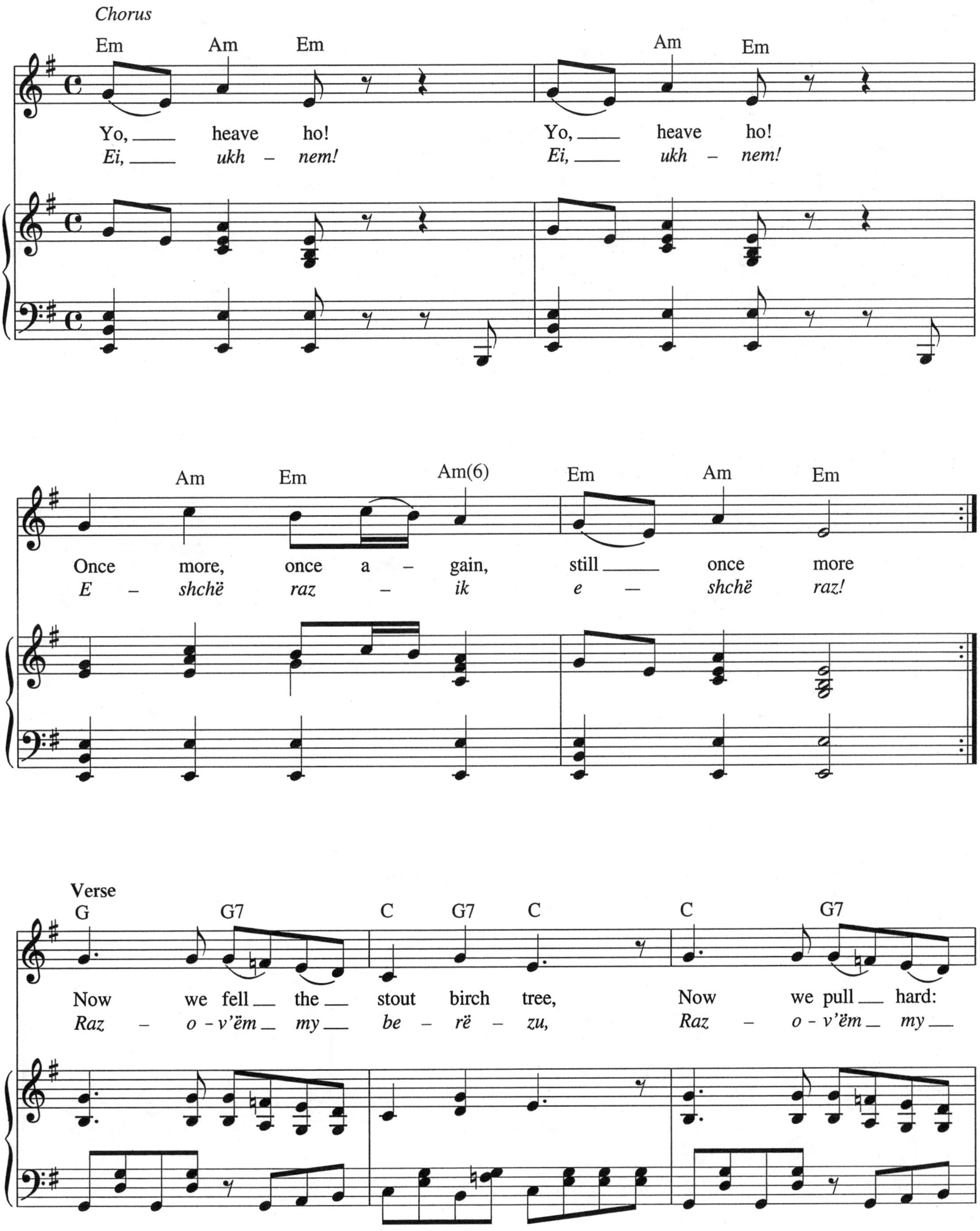

Chorus
Em Am Em Am Em
Yo, heave ho! Yo, heave ho!
Ei, ukh – nem! Ei, ukh – nem!
Am Em Am(6) Em Am Em
Once more, once a – gain, still once more
E – shchë raz – ik e — shchë raz!
Verse
G G7 C G7 C C G7
Now we fell the stout birch tree, Now we pull hard:
Raz – o - v'ëm my be – rë – zu, Raz – o - v'ëm my

one, two, three. Ay da, da, ay da, Ay da, da, ay da,
ku – dria – vu, *Ai da, da, ai da,* *Ai da, da, ai da,*

Now we fell ___ the stout birch tree. Yo, ___ heave ho! Yo, ___ heave ho!
Raz – o – v'ëm ___ my ku – dria – vu. *Ei, ___ ukh – nem!* *Ei, ___ ukh – nem!*

Hey, hey, let's heave a– long the way to the sun ___ we ___ sing ___ our song.
Ei, ei tia – ni ka – nat sme – lei, *Pes – niu sol – nysh – ku po – ëm.*

As the barges float along,
To the sun we sing our song.
Ay-da, da, ay-da!
Ay-da, da, ay-da!
To the sun we sing our song.
Hey, hey, let's heave along the way,
To the sun we sing our song. *Chorus*

Volga, Volga, our pride,
Mighty stream so deep and wide.
Ay-da, da, ay-da!
Ay-da, da, ay-da!
Mighty stream so deep and wide.
Hey, hey, this is why we say
Volga, Volga, you're our pride. *Chorus*

My po berezhku idëm
Pesniu solnyshku poëm,
Ai-da, da, ai-da!
Ai-da, da, ai-da!
Pesniu solnyshku poëm,
Ei, ei tiani kanat smelei,
Pesniu solnyshku poëm. Chorus

Ekh, ty, Volga, mat'-reka,
Shiroka i gluboka.
Ai-da, da, ai-da!
Ai-da, da, ai-da!
Shiroka i gluboka.
Ei, ei chto nam vsevo milei,
Volga, Volga, mat'-reka. Chorus

N.Y. Public Library Picture Collection

Waiting For The Robert E. Lee

1912
Words by L. Wolfe Gilbert
Music by Lewis F. Muir

1. Way down on the lev – ee in old Al – a – bam – y, There's dad–dy and mam—
2. The whis-tles are blow – in', the smoke-stacks are show – in', The ropes they are throw-

— my, there's Eph-raim and Sam – my, On a moon – light night you can find_
— in', ex – cuse me, I'm go – in' to the place where all is har-mon-

— them all. While they are wait – in', the ban–jos are syn – co – pa–tin'.
i – ous, E – ven the preach – er,___ he is the danc – ing teach-er.

What's that they're say – in'?___ What's that they're say – in'?___ While they keep play—
Have you been down__ there? __ Were you a – round__ there? If ev – er you go_

in', ___ Hum-min' and sway – in', It's the good ship

there, you'll al – ways be found ___ there, why, dog – gone! here

Rob-ert E. Lee, ___ that's come to car–ry the cot–ton a – way. ___

comes ___ my ba ___ by on the good old ___ *Rob-ert E. Lee.* ___

Chorus

Watch them shuf – flin' a – long, ___ See them shuf – flin' a –

long. ___ Go take your best gal, real pal, Go

down to the lev – ee, I said to the lev – ee, And join that shuf-

– lin' throng, Hear that mu – sic and

song. It's sim–ply great, mate, wait–in' on the

lev – ee, wait–in' for the *Rob–ert* *E.* *Lee.*

Hudson River Steamboat

A picture of 19th-century life on the Hudson River: busy river traffic from New York to Albany . . . shad fishermen (a major occupation) . . . pickle boats from Yonkers supplying New York City's ever-growing demand . . . steamboat races . . . .

Choo – choo to slack 'er, Pack - et - boat, tow - boat and a doub- le stack- er,

Choo-choo to Tar- ry- town, Spuy-ten Duy-vil all a-round. Choo-choo to go a – head, choo-choo to back 'er.

Shad boat, pickle boat, lying side by side,
Fisherfolk and sailormen, waiting for the tide,
Rain cloud, storm cloud over yonder hill,
Thunder on the Dunderberg, rumbles in the kill. *Chorus*

The *Sedgewick* was racing and she lost all hope,
Used up her steam on the big calliope,
But she hopped right along, she was hopping quick,
All the way from Stony Point up to Pappaloppen Crick.

Final Chorus:
Choo, choo to go ahead,
Choo, choo to slack 'er,
Packet-boat, tow-boat and a double stacker.
New York to Albany, Rondout and Tivoli,
Choo, choo to go ahead,
And choo, choo to back 'er.

N.Y. Public Library Picture Collection

Backwater Blues

Well, it rained five days and the sky turned black as night. __

Yes, it rained five days and the sky turned black as night. __

There was trou-ble tak–ing place in the low-lands that night. __

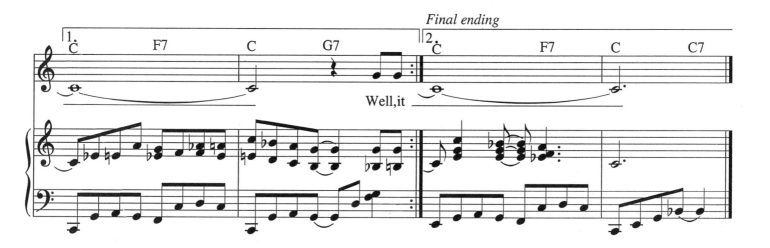

Well, it

Well, it thundered and it lightened and the winds began to blow, (2)
There was thousands of people didn't have no place to go.

I woke up this morning, couldn't even get out my door, (2)
Enough trouble to make a poor boy wonder where he gonna go.

I went out to the lonesome, high old lonesome hill, (2)
And looked down on the old house where I used to live.

Backwater blues have caused me to pack up my things and go, (2)
'Cause my house fell down and I can't live there no more.

N.Y. Public Library Picture Collection

Deep River Blues

Let it rain, ___   let it pour, ___   Let it rain ___   a
Let the rain, ___   drive right on, ___   Let the waves ___   just

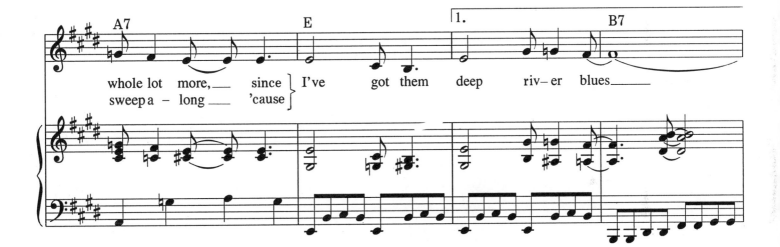

whole lot more, ___   since   I've   got them   deep   riv–er   blues ___
sweep a – long ___   'cause

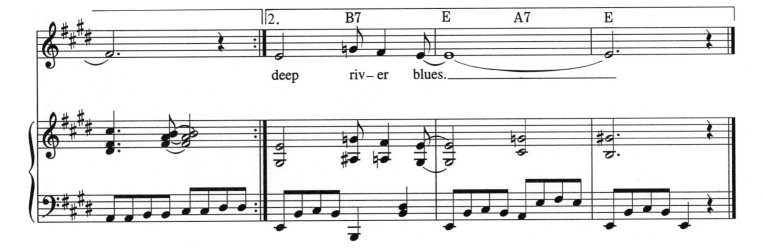

deep   riv–er   blues. ___

My old gal's a good old pal,
She looks just like a waterfowl,
When I get them deep-river blues,
There ain't no one to cry for me,
And the fish all go out on a spree,
When I get them deep-river blues.

Give me back my old boat,
I'm gonna sail, if she'll float,
'Cause I've got them deep-river blues.
I'm goin' back to Muscle Shoals,
Times are better there, I'm told,
'Cause I've got them deep-river blues.

If my boat sinks with me,
I'll go down, don't you see,
'Cause I've got them deep-river blues.
Now I'm goin' to say good-bye,
And if I sink just let me die,
'Cause I've got them deep-river blues.

N.Y. Public Library Picture Collection

163

The Jam On Gerry's Rock

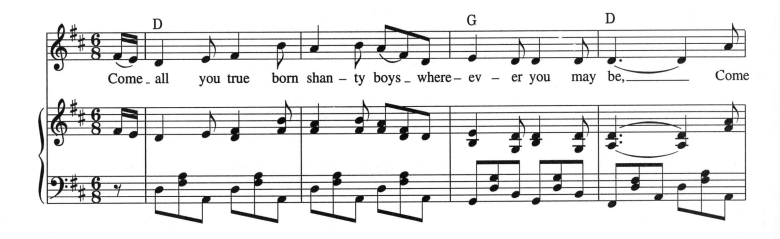

Come all you true born shan – ty boys where – ev – er you may be,_____ Come

sit you on the dea – con seat___ and list – en un – to___ me._____ I'll

sing the jam on Ger – ry's Rock and a he – ro you___ should know;_____ The

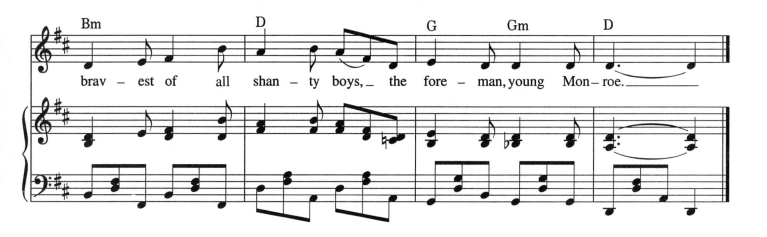

brav – est of all shan – ty boys, _ the fore – man, young Mon – roe. _____

'Twas on a Sunday morning,
Ere daylight did appear,
The logs were piling mountain-high:
We could not keep them clear.
"Cheer up! Cheer up, my rivermen,
Relieve your hearts of woe!
We'll break the jam on Gerry's Rock!"
Cried our foreman, young Monroe.

Now some of them were willing,
While others hid from sight.
To break a jam on Sunday
They did not think it right.
Till six of our brave shanty-boys
Did volunteer to go
And break the jam on Gerry's Rock
With our foreman, young Monroe.

They had not picked off many logs
Till Monroe to them did say,
"I must send you back up the drive, my boys,
For the jam will soon give way!"
Alone he freed the key-log then,
And when the jam did go,
It carried away on the boiling flood
Our foreman, young Monroe.

Now when the boys up at the camp
The news they came to hear,
In search of his dead body
Down the river they did steer;
And there they found to their surprise,
Their sorrow, grief, and woe,
All bruised and mangled on the beach
Lay the corpse of young Monroe.

They picked him up most tenderly,
Smoothed down his raven hair.
There was one among the watchers
Whose cries did rend the air.
The fairest lass of Saginaw
Let tears of anguish flow;
But her moans and cries could not awake
Her true love, young Monroe.

The Missus Clark, a widow,
Lived by the riverside;
This was her only daughter,
Monroe's intended bride.
So the wages of her perished love
The boss to her did pay
And a gift of gold was sent to her
By the shanty-boys next day.

When she received the money
She thanked them tearfully,
But it was not her portion
Long on the earth to be;
For it was just six weeks or so
When she was called to go,
And the shanty-boys laid her at rest
By the side of young Monroe.

They decked the graves most decently—
'Twas on the fourth of May;
Come all ye true-born shanty-boys
And for a comrade pray!
Engraven on a hemlock tree
Which by the beach did grow,
Are the name and date of the mournful fate
Of the foreman, young Monroe.

Rock About, My Saro Jane

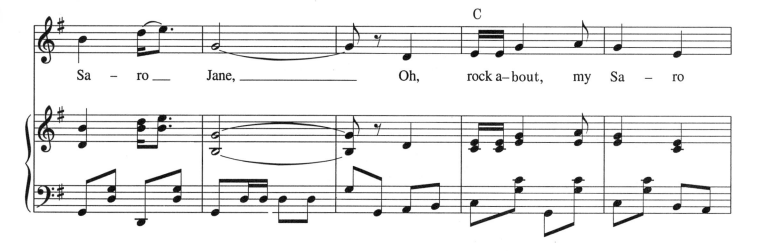

Sa - ro __ Jane, _____ Oh, rock a–bout, my Sa - ro

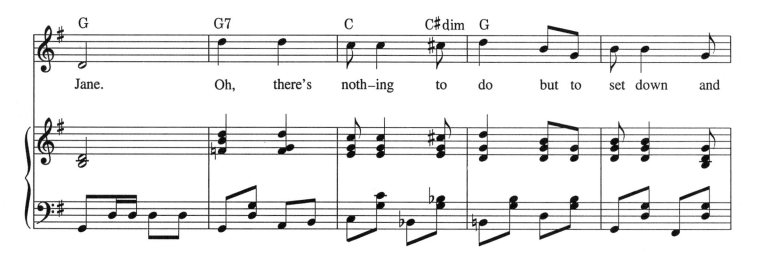

Jane. Oh, there's noth–ing to do but to set down and

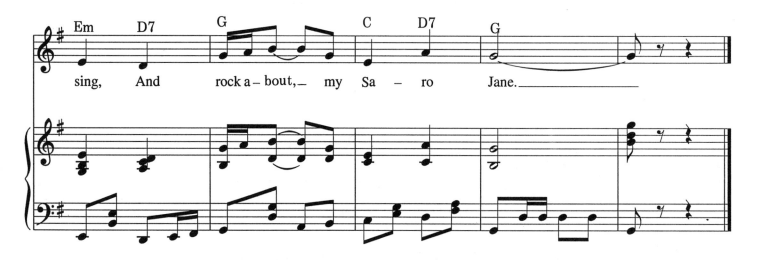

sing, And rock a–bout,_ my Sa - ro Jane._____

Biler busted and the whistle done blowed,
The head captain done fell overboard.
O Saro Jane! *Chorus*

Engine gave a crack and the whistle gave a squall,
The engineer gone to the hole in the wall.
O Saro Jane! *Chorus*

Yankees built boats for to shoot them rebels,
My musket's loaded and I'm gonna hold her level.
O Saro Jane! *Chorus*

Rio Grande

Oh say, were you ev – er in Ri – o Grande? Way _____ oh

Ri – o. _____ It's there that the riv – er flows down gold – en sand, And we're

bound for the Ri – o Grande. Then a – way, love, _ a –

way. Way_____ oh Ri – o._____ So

fare__ ye well,__ my pret–ty young gal, And we're bound for the Ri – o Grande._____

And good-bye, fare you well, all you ladies of town...
We've left you enough for to buy a silk gown.... *Chorus*

So it's pack up your donkey and get under way...
The girls we are leaving can take our half-pay.... *Chorus*

Now you Bowery ladies, we'd have you to know...
We're bound to Southward, O Lord, let us go.... *Chorus*

The Blues Ain't Nothin'

"That river" might have been any one of the dozens of Texas streams. Big ones like the Red River, Colorado River, Canadian River, Rio Grande—smaller ones like the Trinity, Brazos, Navasota, Neches, Navidad.

I'm gon—na build my – self a raft_____ And float that ri – ver

down._____ I'll build my – self a shack in

some old Tex – as town. Mmm___ mmm___ 'Cause the

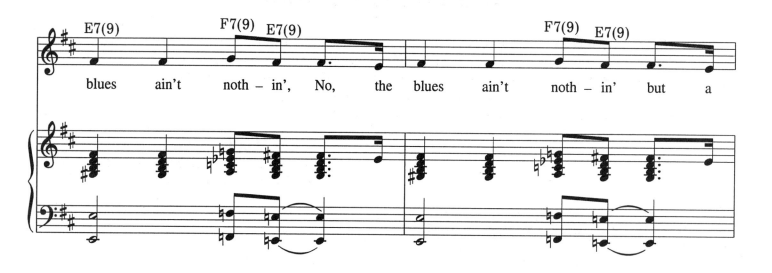

blues ain't noth – in', No, the blues ain't noth – in' but a

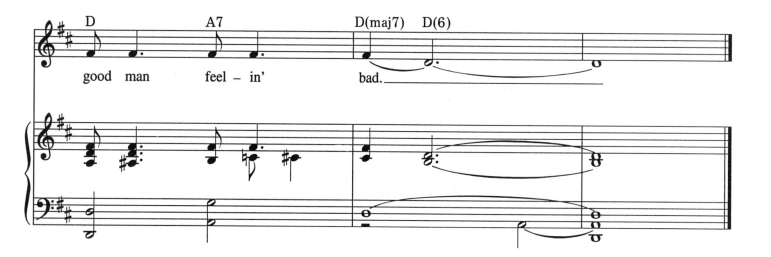

good man feel – in' bad._____

I'm goin' down on the levee,
Goin' to take myself a rockin' chair.
If my lovin' gal don't come,
I'll rock away from there.
Mmm-mmm...
'Cause the blues ain't nothin',
No, the blues ain't nothin'
But a good man feelin' bad.

Why did you leave me blue?
Why did you leave me blue?
All I can do is sit
And cry and cry for you.
Mmm-mmm...
'Cause the blues ain't nothin',
No, the blues ain't nothin'
But a good man feelin' bad.

Roll On, Columbia

In May 1941, Woody Guthrie was invited by the Bonneville Power Administration to come to Columbia River country, take a look around, and make up some songs about the Grand Coulee Dam and the Bonneville Dam. It was exactly the right kind of task for the man who was later to compose "This Land Is Your Land" and hundreds of other songs about America, written from the working man's perspective. The following three songs are taken from the 26 that Woody composed along the Columbia River.

Words by Woody Guthrie
Music Based on "GOODNIGHT IRENE"
by Huddie Ledbetter and John A. Lomax

Green doug–las fir where the wat–er cuts through, Down the wild can–yons and val–leys she flew Pa–ci–fic North–west to the o–cean so blue, It's roll on, Co–lum–bia, roll on.

Roll on, Co - lum - bia, roll on,

Roll on, Co - lum - bia, roll on; your

pow - er is turn - ing the dark - ness to dawn — It's

roll on, Co - lum - bia, roll on.

Other great rivers add power to you,
Yakima, Snake, and the Klickitat, too,
Sandy, Willamette, and Hood River, too;
Roll on, Columbia, roll on! *Chorus*

Tom Jefferson's vision would not let him rest,
An empire he saw in the Pacific Northwest.
Sent Lewis and Clark and they did the rest;
Roll on Columbia, roll on! *Chorus*

It's there on your banks that we fought many a fight;
Sheridan's boys in the block house that night,
They saw us in death, but never in flight;
Roll on, Columbia, roll on! *Chorus*

At Bonneville now there are ships in the locks,
The waters have risen and cleared all the rocks,
Shiploads of plenty will steam past the docks,
So, roll on, Columbia, roll on! *Chorus*

And on up the river at Grand Coulee Dam,
The mightiest thing ever built by a man,
To run the great factories for old Uncle Sam;
It's roll on, Columbia, roll on! *Chorus*

N.Y. Public Library Picture Collection

N.Y. Public Library Picture Collection

Talking Columbia Blues

**Words and Music
By Woody Guthrie**

Filled up my hatbrim, drunk a little taste,
Thought about a river just a-goin' to waste,
Thought about the dust, thought about the sand,
Thought about the people, thought about the land.
    Folks a-running around. Lookin' for a little place.

You just watch this river, and pretty soon
Everybody's a-going to change their tune,
The big Grand Coulee and the Bonneville Dam,
Run a thousand factories for Uncle Sam.
    Everything from fertilizer to sewing machines.
    Atomic bedrooms and plastic—everything's goin' to be plastic.

Well, I pulled out my pencil and I scribbled this song,
Figured all of them salmon just couldn't be wrong;
Them salmon fish is pretty shrewd,
They got senators and politicians, too.
    Just like a President—run every four years.

Uncle Sam needs houses and stuff to eat,
Uncle Sam needs wool, Uncle Sam needs wheat,
Uncle Sam needs water and power dams,
Uncle Sam needs people and the people need land.
    Don't like dictators—but the whole country'd
    ought to be run by electricity.

The Ballad Of The Great Grand Coulee Dam

"I saw the Columbia River and the big Grand Coulee Dam from just about every cliff, mountain, tree, and post from which it can be seen. I made up 26 songs about the Columbia and about the dam and about the men, and these songs were recorded by the Department of the Interior, Bonneville Power Administration out in Portland. The records were played at all sorts and sizes of meetings where people bought bonds to bring the power lines over the fields and hills to their own little places. Electricity to milk the cows, kiss the maid, shoe the old mare, light up the saloon, the chili joint window, the schools, and churches along the way, to run the factories turning out manganese, chrome, bauxite, aluminum, and steel." (Woody Guthrie)

By Woody Guthrie

Now the world has sev – en won–ders that the trav–'llers al – ways tell, Some gar – dens and some tow – ers, I guess you know them well. But now the great–est won – der is in Un – cle Sam's fair land; It's the

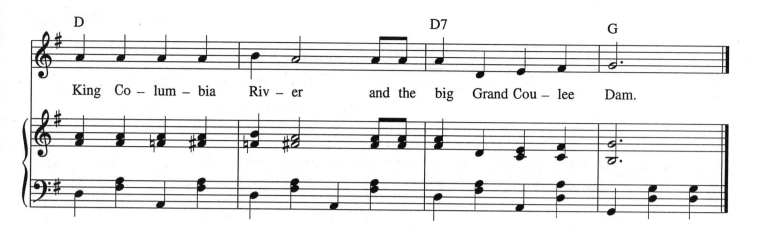

King Co – lum – bia Riv – er and the big Grand Cou – lee Dam.

She heads up the Canadian mountains where the rippling waters glide,
Comes a-rumbling down the canyon, to meet the salty tide
Of the wide Pacific Ocean where the sun sets in the west,
And the big Grand Coulee country in the land I love the best.

At the Umatilla Rapids, at The Dalles, and at Cascades,
Mighty men have carved a history of the sacrifices made,
In the thundering foaming waters of the big Celilo Falls,
In the big Grand Coulee country that I love the best of all.

She winds down the granite canyon, and she bends across the lea,
Like a prancing dancing stallion down her seaway to the sea;
Cast your eyes upon the biggest thing yet built by human hands,
On the King Columbia River, it's the big Grand Coulee Dam.

In the misty crystal glitter of the wild and windward spray,
Men have fought the pounding waters, and met a watery grave,
Well she tore their boats to splinters and she gave men dreams to dream,
Of the day the Coulee Dam would cross that wild and wasted stream.

There at Bonneville on the river is a green and beautiful sight,
See the Bonneville Dam a-rising in the sun so clear and white;
While the leaping salmon play along the ladder and the rocks,
There's a steamboat load of gasoline a-whistling in the locks.

Uncle Sam took up the challenge in the year of thirty-three,
For the farmer and the worker, and all of you and me,
He said roll along, Columbia, you can ramble to the sea,
But river, while you're rambling, you can do some work for me.

Now in Washington and Oregon you hear the fact'ries hum,
Making chrome and making manganese and light aluminum,
And the roaring flying fortress wings her way for Uncle Sam,
Spawned upon the King Columbia by the big Grand Coulee Dam.

A Trip On The River

By Jerry Silverman

Would-n't you like to take a trip on the riv-er?
Would-n't you like to catch a fish on the riv-er?

Just like we used to __ do?

Would-n't you like to sail a ship on the riv-er?
Would-n't you like to make a wish on the riv-er?

I would, would-n't __ you?

I would, would-n't you? Oh,

would-n't you like to know there's hope for the riv-er? Know that the peo-ple care?____

180

Wouldn't you like to take a swim in the river?...
Wouldn't you like to plunge right into the river?...
  Wouldn't you like to take a drink from the river?...
  Wouldn't you like to stop and think by the river?... *Chorus*

Wouldn't you like to see kids play by the river?...
Wouldn't you like to spend a day by the river?...
  Wouldn't you like to meet a friend by the river?...
  Wouldn't you like to stroll the bend of the river?... *Chorus*

Wouldn't you like to come along to the river?...
Wouldn't you like to sing a song on the river?...
  Wouldn't you like to see wild geese by the river?...
  Wouldn't you like to live in peace by the river?... *Chorus*

How Are We Going To Save Tomorrow?
(The PCB Song)

"Here's more songs from that starry-eyed gang that thinks you can start to start saving a river if you sail a beautiful boat up and down it. We use songs to make the work go easier, we use songs to bring a crowd down to the water's edge that had been abandoned. We sing of days gone by, but also of days we are sure will come, when the fish are again safe to eat, the upriver water is safe to drink, and all of it will be fine swimming for young and old.

Why are we so sure? Well, it can happen in one of two ways. Either the world learns how to get along, and we get rid of war, poverty, racism, sexism, and pollution. Or we don't get rid of war, poverty, racism, sexism, and pollution—in which case we'll be back in the stone age—if we're lucky—and the few surviving humans won't be able to pollute much.

We hope that *Clearwater's* message will be heard across the land, and help sailors in many other lakes, bays, rivers, to make of their boats not a private escape, but a tool for public enlightenment, and citizen action.

And singing will help.

(Pete Seeger, *The Clearwater Songbook,* 1980)

**Words and Music
By Pete Seeger**

crime, But how are we gon-na save to – mor–row? _____

The river was looking cleaner, it started to get clear,
We looked forward to the fishing getting better every year.
But now the scientists tell us things are not as they appear.
How are we gonna save tomorrow? *Chorus*

The experts knew about it; so why not you and me?
Who controls the information in this land of the free?
In seventy-two they told us law and order was the key,
How are we gonna save tomorrow? *Chorus*

Here's to the canary that we took down in the mine.
Here's to the Hudson striper, may his warning come in time.
Here's to all the young folks singing, "This land is yours and mine!"
That's how we're gonna save tomorrow. *Chorus II*

Chorus II:
Don't throw away that shad net; don't junk that hook and line.
We can build a better world; we can start in time.
Clearwater, Clearwater, this land is you and me,
And somehow we're gonna save tomorrow.

The longest journey taken needs a first step to begin.
The world wasn't given us to lose, we've got a world to win.
Clearwater says to lend a hand, a paw, a wing, a fin.
All together, we can save tomorrow. *Chorus II*

185

. . . Lakes . . .

The Persia's Crew

Sad and dis - mal is the tale I will re - late to you,_____ A-

bout the schoon - er *Per - sia,* her of - fi - cers and crew,_____ Who

sank be - neath the storm - y deep, in life to rise no more,_____ When

winds and des - o - la - tion swept lake Hu - ron's rock - bound shore._____

They left Chicago on their lee, their songs they did resound,
And they so full of joy and glee as homeward they were
   bound.
They little thought the sound of death would meet them on
   their way,
And they, so full of joy and glee, should in Lake Huron lay.

The sailors' names I did not know, excepting one or two.
Down in the deep they all did go; they were a luckless crew.
Not a soul escaped to land to clear the myst'ry o'er;
In watery depths they all did go, upon Lake Huron's shore.

In mystery their dooms are sealed; they did collide, some say,
But that is all to be revealed upon the judgment day,
And when the angels take their stand to wake the waters blue,
And send forth the commander of the ill-starred *Persia's*
   crew.

Daniel Sullivan was their mate, a man both bold and brave,
As ever was compelled by fate to fill a sailor's grave.
He will be mourned as a friend; alas! his days are o'er.
In watery depths, he now doth lie, upon Lake Huron's shore.

Oh, Dan, your many friends will mourn, your fate upon them
   frown;
They'll wait in vain for your return back in Oswego town.
They'll miss the sly glance of your eye, your hand they'll clasp
   no more;
In watery depths you now do lie, upon Lake Huron's shore.

No mother's hand was there to press that brow-distracting pain;
No gentle wife was there to kiss that cold brow o'er again.
No sister or no brother nigh, no little ones to mourn;
Down in the deep they all did go, far from their friends and
   home.

Around Presque Isle the seagulls scream their dismal notes along,
And that is the sad requiem of the dismal funeral song.
They skim along the water blue, and then aloft they soar,
In memory of the *Persia's* crew, lost on Lake Huron's shore.

The Bigler

According to the story, the *Bigler* was the slowest vessel on the Great Lakes. You can plot its course from Milwaukee to Detroit from verse to verse. "Wabbleshanks," in the fourth verse, is sailorese for Waugoshance Point, at the entrance to the Straits of Makinac ("Makinaw")—heading east from Lake Michigan into Lake Huron.

Come all my boys and lis-ten, ____ a song I'll sing to you. ____ It's all a-bout the *Big-ler* ____ and of her jol-ly crew. In Mil-wau-kee last Oc—

free, On our down trip to Buf-fa-lo___ from Mil – wau – kee.

It was on one Sunday morning, just at the hour of ten,
When the *Nickle Roberts* towed the *Bigler* into Lake Michigan.
O there we made our canvas in the middle of the fleet,
O the wind hauled to the south'ard, boys, and we had to give her sheet. *Chorus*

The wind come down from the sou' sou'-west, it blowed both stiff and strong,
You had orter seen the *Bigler*, as she plowed Lake Michigan,
O far beyant her foaming bows the fiery waves to fling,
With every stitch of canvas and her course was sing and wing. *Chorus*

We made Beaver Head Light and Wabbleshanks, the entrance to the straits,
And might have passed the whole fleet there, if they'd hove to and wait,
But we drove them all before us the nicest you ever saw,
Clear out into Lake Huron through the Straits of Mackinaw. *Chorus*

First, Forty Mile Point and Presque Isle Light, and then we boomed away,
The wind being fresh and fair, for the Isle of Thunder Bay;
The wind it shifted to a close haul, all on the starboard tack,
With a good lookout ahead we made for Point Aubarques. *Chorus*

We made the Light and kept in sight of Michigan's east shore
A-booming for the river as we'd often done before,
And when abreast Port Huron Light, our small anchor we let go,
The tug *Kate Moffet* came along and took the *Bigler* in tow. *Chorus*

The *Moffet* took six schooners in tow, and all of us fore and aft,
She took us down to Lake Saint Claire and stuck us on the flat,
She parted the *Hunter's* towline in trying to give relief,
And stem to stern went the *Bigler*, smash into the *Mapleleaf. Chorus*

Then she towed us through and left us outside the river light,
Lake Erie for to wander and the blustering winds to fight,
The wind was from the sou'west, and we paddled our own canoe,
Her jib boom pointed the Dummy, she's hellbent for Buffalo. *Chorus*

Red Iron Ore

Come all you bold sail – ors that fol – low the Lakes On an i – ron ore ves – sel your

liv – ing to make; I shipped in Chi – ca – go, bid a – dieu to the shore, Bound a –

way to Es – ca – na – ba for red i – ron ore. Der – ry down, down, down der – ry down.

In the month of September, the seventeenth day,
Two dollars and a quarter is all they would pay,
And on Monday morning the *Bridgeport* did take
The *E. C. Roberts* out in the Lake. *Chorus*

The wind from the south'ard sprang up a fresh breeze,
And away through Lake Michigan the *Roberts* did sneeze.
Down through Lake Michigan the *Roberts* did roar,
And on Friday morning we passed through death's door. *Chorus*

This packet she howled across the mouth of Green Bay,
And before her cutwater she dashed the white spray.
We rounded the sand point, out anchor let go,
We furled in our canvas and the watch went below. *Chorus*

Next morning we hove alongside the *Exile,*
And soon was made fast to an iron ore pile,
They lowered their duties and like thunder did roar,
They spouted into us that red iron ore. *Chorus*

Some sailors took shovels while others got spades,
And some took wheelbarrows, each man to his trade.
We looked like red devils, our fingers got sore,
We cursed *Escanaba* and that damned iron ore. *Chorus*

The tug *Escanaba* she towed out the *Minch,*
The *Roberts* she thought she had left in a pinch,
And as she passed by us she bid us good-bye,
Saying, "We'll meet you in Cleveland next Fourth of July!" *Chorus*

Through Louse Island it blew a fresh breeze;
We made the Foxes, the Beavers, the Skillagelees;
We flew by the *Minch* for to show her the way,
And she ne'er hove in sight till we were off Thunder Bay. *Chorus*

Across Saginaw Bay the *Roberts* did ride
With the dark and deep water rolling over her side.
And now for Port Huron the *Roberts* must go,
Where the tug *Kate Williams* she took us in tow. *Chorus*

We went through North Passage—O Lord, how it blew!
And all 'round the Dummy a large fleet there came too.
The night being dark, Old Nick it would scare.
We hove up next morning and for Cleveland did steer. *Chorus*

Now the *Roberts* is in Cleveland, made fast stem and stern,
And over bottle we'll spin a big yarn.
But Captain Harvey Shannon had ought to stand treat
For getting into Cleveland ahead of the fleet. *Chorus*

Now my song is ended, I hope you won't laugh.
Our dunnage is packed and all hands are paid off.
Here's a health to the *Roberts,* she's staunch, strong and true;
Not forgotten the bold boys that comprise her crew. *Chorus*

The Wreck Of The Edmond Fitzgerald

By Gordon Lightfoot

The ship was the pride of the American side
Coming back from some mill in Wisconsin.
As the big freighters go it was bigger than most
With a crew and good captain well seasoned.

Concluding some terms with a couple of steel firms
When they left fully loaded for Cleveland,
And later that night when the ship's bell rang,
Could it be the north wind they'd been feelin'?

The wind in the wires made a tattletale sound
And a wave broke over the railing.
And every man knew as the captain did, too,
'Twas the witch of November come stealin'.

The dawn came late and the breakfast had to wait
When the Gales of November came slashin'.
When afternoon came it was freezin' rain
In the face of a hurricane west wind.

When suppertime came the old cook came on deck
Sayin', "Fellas, it's too rough t'feed ya."
At seven p.m. a main hatchway caved in;
He said, "Fellas, it's bin good t'know ya."

The captain wired in he had water comin' in
And the good ship and crew was in peril.
And later that night when 'is lights went outta sight
Came the wreck of the *Edmund Fitzgerald*.

Does anyone know where the love of God goes
When the waves turn the minutes to hours.
The searchers all say they'd have made Whitefish Bay
If they'd put fifteen more miles behind 'er.

They might have split up or they might have capsized;
They may have broke deep and took water,
And all that remains is the faces and the names
Of the wives and the sons and the daughters.

Lake Huron rolls, Superior swings
In the rooms of her ice-water mansion.
Old Michigan steams like a young man's dreams;
The islands and bays are for sportsmen.

And farther below Lake Ontario
Takes in what Lake Erie can send her.
And the iron boats go as the mariners all know
With the Gales of November remembered.

In a musty old hall in Detroit they prayed
In the Maritime Sailors' Cathedral.
The church bell chimed 'til it rang twenty-nine times
For each man on the *Edmund Fitzgerald*.

The legend lives on from the Chippewa on down
Of the big lake they called "Gitchee Gumee."
"Superior," they said, "never gives up her dead
When the Gales of November come early!"

. . . And Canals

The E-Ri-E Canal

Twenty years after New York Governor De Witt Clinton floated down the newly opened Erie Canal on the *Sequoia Chief* from Buffalo to Albany and down the Hudson River to New York harbor in 1825, Michigan had increased its population by 60 times, and Ohio had climbed from 13th to the 3rd most heavily populated state in the Union. The Erie Canal was the highway for most of these settlers and their goods. Clinton's 425-mile ditch had proved itself. New York was, indeed, the Empire State.

We were for-ty miles from Al-ba-ny, For-get it I nev-er

shall, What a ter-ri-ble storm we had one night On the E-ri-e Ca-

Chorus

nal. Oh, the E-ri-e was a-ris-in' And the gin was a-get-tin'

low,   And I scarce–ly think we'll get a drink, Till we

get to Buf–fa–lo–o–o, Till we get to Buf–fa–lo.

We were loaded down with barley,
We were chock full up on rye,
And the captain he looked down at me
With his gol-durn' wicked eye. *Chorus*

The captain he came up on deck
With a spyglass in his hand.
And the fog it was so gosh-darn thick,
That he could not spy the land. *Chorus*

Two days out of Syracuse
Our vessel struck a shoal,
And we like to all been drownded
On a chunk o' Lackawanna coal. *Chorus*

Our cook she was a grand old gal,
She wore a ragged dress.
We hoisted her upon a pole
As a signal of distress. *Chorus*

The captain, he got married,
And the cook, she went to jail.
And I'm the only son of a gun
That's left to tell the tale. *Chorus*

Low Bridge!-Everybody Down
(Fifteen Years On The Erie Canal)

By Thomas S. Allen (1913)

We better be on our way old pal,
Fifteen miles on the Erie Canal.
'Cause you bet your life I'd never part from Sal,
Fifteen miles on the Erie Canal.
Get up there, mule, here comes a lock,
We'll make Rome 'bout six o'clock.
One more trip and back we'll go,
Right back home to Buffalo. *Chorus*

Oh, where would I be if I lost my pal?
Fifteen years on the Erie Canal,
Oh, I'd like to see a mule as good as Sal,
Fifteen years on the Erie Canal.
A friend of mine once got her sore,
Now he's got a broken jaw.
'Cause she let fly with her iron toe
And kicked him into Buffalo.

Chorus:
Low bridge, everybody down,
Low bridge, I've got the finest mule in town,
If you're looking 'round for trouble, better stay away from Sal,
She's the only fighting donkey on the Erie Canal.

I don't have to call when I want my Sal,
Fifteen years on the Erie Canal;
She trots from her stall like a good old gal,
Fifteen years on the Erie Canal.
I eat my meals with Sal each day,
I eat beef and she eats hay,
She ain't so slow if you want to know,
She put the "Buff" in Buffalo.

Chorus:
Low bridge, everybody down,
Low bridge, I've got the finest mule in town,
Eats a bale of hay for dinner, and on top of that, my Sal
Tries to drink up all the water in the Erie Canal.

You'll soon hear them sing all about my gal,
Fifteen years on the Erie Canal,
It's a darned fool ditty 'bout my darned fool Sal,
Fifteen years on the Erie Canal.
Oh, every band will play it soon,
Darned fool words and darned fool tune;
You'll hear it sung everywhere you go;
From Mexico to Buffalo.

Chorus:
Low bridge, everybody down,
Low bridge, I've got the finest mule in town,
She's a perfect, perfect lady, and she blushes like a gal,
If she hears you sing about her and the Erie Canal.

N.Y. Public Library Picture Collection

A Trip On The Erie

You yacht on the Hud-son, you ride on the Lake, But a trip on the E-rie, you bet, takes the cake. Where the beef-steak is tough as a fight-ing dog's neck, And the cook she plays tag with the flies on the deck.

Our cook is a daisy and dead stuck on me,
Has fiery red hair and she's sweet sixty-three.
Though sunburned and freckled, a daisy, you bet,
And we use her at night for a headlight on deck.

So haul in your towline and take in your slack,
Take a reef in your breeches and straighten your back.
Through sunshine and storm down the towpath we'll walk,
And we'll touch up the mules when the kick and they balk.

The Raging Can-all

Slowly, with mock seriousness

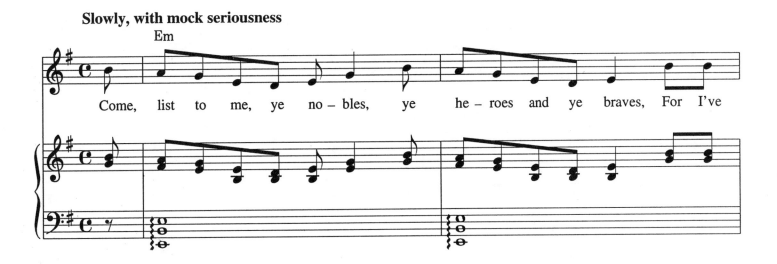

Come, list to me, ye no-bles, ye he-roes and ye braves, For I've

been___ at the mer-cy of the winds___ and the waves. I'll tell you of the hard-ships to

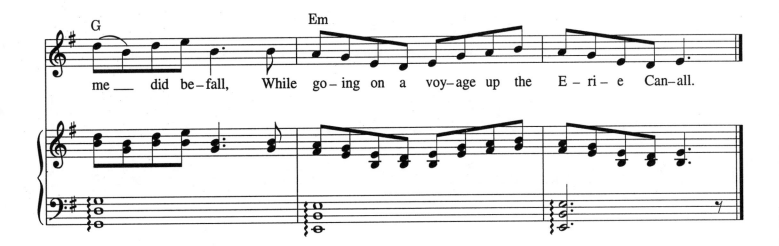

me ___ did be-fall, While go-ing on a voy-age up the E-ri-e Can-all.

From out of this famed harbor we sailed without fear,
Our helm we put hard up, and for Albany did steer,
We spoke full fifty craft, without any accident at all
Until we passed into that 'ere raging can-all.

We left old Albany harbor, just at the close of day,
If rightly I remember 'twas the second day of May;
We trusted to our driver, although he was but small,
Yet he knew all the windings of that raging can-all.

It seemed as if the devil had work in hands that night,
For our oil was all out, and our lamps they gave no light:
The clouds began to gather, and the rain began to fall,
And I wished myself off and safe from the raging can-all.

With hearts chock-full of love, we thought of our sweethearts
  dear,
And straight for Utica our gallant bark did steer,
When in sight of that 'ere town, there came on a white squall,
Which carried away our mizzenmast, on the raging can-all.

The winds came roaring on, just like a wildcat scream,
Our little vessel pitched and tos'd, straining every beam,
The cook she drop'd the bucket, and let the ladle fall,
And the waves ran mountains high, on the raging can-all.

Now the weather being foggy we couldn't see the track,
We made our driver come on board, and hitched a lantern on
  his back.
We told him to be fearless, and when it blew a gale,
To jump *up* and knock *down* a horse, that's taking in a sail.

The captain bid the driver to hurry with all speed,
His orders were obeyed, for he soon cracked up his lead;
With that 'ere kind of towing, he allowed by twelve o'clock
We should have the old critter right bang agin the dock.

But sad was the fate of our poor devoted bark,
For the rain kept growing faster, and the night it grew dark,
The horses gave a stumble, and the driver gave a squall,
And they tumbled head and heels into the raging can-all.

The captain cried out, with a voice so clear and sound,
"Cut them horses loose, my boys, or else we will be drowned!"
The driver paddled to the shore, although he was but small,
While the horses sank to rise no more in the raging can-all.

The cook she wrung her hands, and then she came on deck,
Saying, "Alas! what will become of us, our vessel is a wreck."
The steersman knocked her over, for he was a man of sense,
And the helmsman jumped ashore, and lashed her to a fence.

We had a load of Dutch, and stowed 'em in the hole,
And the varmints wer'nt the least concerned for the welfare of
  their souls:
The captain he went down to them, implored them for to pray,
But all the answer that he got was "Due deutsch sproken, nex
  come arouse, ex for shtae."

The captain trembled for his money, likewise for his wife,
But to muster courage up, he whittled with a knife,
He said to us with a faltering voice, while tears began to fall,
"Prepare to meet your death this night on the raging can-all."

The passengers to save their souls would part with any
  money,
The bar-keeper went on his knees, then took some peach and
  honey;
A lady took some brandy, she'd have it neat or not at all,
Kase there was lots of water in the raging can-all.

The captain came on deck, with spyglass in his hand,
But the fog it was 'tarnel thick, he couldn't spy the land;
He put his trumpet to his mouth, as loud as he could bawl
He hailed for assistance from the raging can-all.

The sky was rent asunder, the lightning it did flash,
The thunder rattled above, just like eternal smash;
The clouds were all upsot, and the rigging it did fall,
And we scudded under bare poles on that raging can-all.

A mighty sea rolled on astern, and then it swept our deck,
And soon our gallant little craft was but a floating wreck;
All hands sprang forward, aft the main-sheet for to haul,
When slap dash! went our chicken coop into the raging can-
  all.

We took the old cook's petticoat, for want of a better dress,
And rigged it out upon a pole, a signal of distress;
We pledged ourselves hand to hand, aboard the boat to bide,
And not to quit the deck while a plank hung to her side.

At length that horrid night cut dirt from the sky,
The storm it did abate, and a boat came passing by,
She soon espied our signal, while each on his knees did fall,
Thankful we escaped a grave on the raging can-all.

We each of us took a nip, and signed the pledge anew,
And wonderful, as danger ceased, how up our courage grew;
The craft in sight bore down on us, and quickly was 'long side,
And we all jumped aboard, and for Buffalo did ride.

And if I live a thousand years, the horrors of that night
Will ever in my memory be, a spot most burning bright;
There's not in this varsal world can ever raise my gall
As the thoughts of my voyage on that raging can-all.

And now, my boys, I'll tell you how to manage wind and
  weather:
In a storm hug the towpath, and lay feather to feather,
And when the weather gets bad, and rain begins to fall,
Jump right ashore, and streak it from the raging can-all.

The yarn is rather long, my boys, so I will let it drop,
You can get the whole particulars in comic Elton's shop,
At eighteen in Division Street you've only got to call,
And you'll get an extra dose of the raging can-all.

The Old Canal

The Ohio and Erie Canal joined Lake Erie in the north with the Ohio River in the south. The canal went into operation in 1827 and opened both the New York and New Orleans markets to Ohio producers. Traffic on the Erie Canal reached its peak in the 1850s, but by the turn of the century the railroads had practically put it out of business, and it was closed in 1913.

There's a lit – tle sil – ver rib – bon runs a – cross the Buck-eye State, 'Tis the

dear-est place of all this earth to me, For up – on its pla-cid sur-face I was

born some years a – go, And its beau-ty, gran-deur, al – ways I do see.

Cleve–land is the north–ern end and Ports–mouth is the south, While its

side cuts they are man-y, man-y, Pal. And where- e'er we went we took a – long our

home, sweet home, you know, In those bal–my days up – on the old ca – nal. There's

naught in all cre – a – tion that to this can com–pare, Good

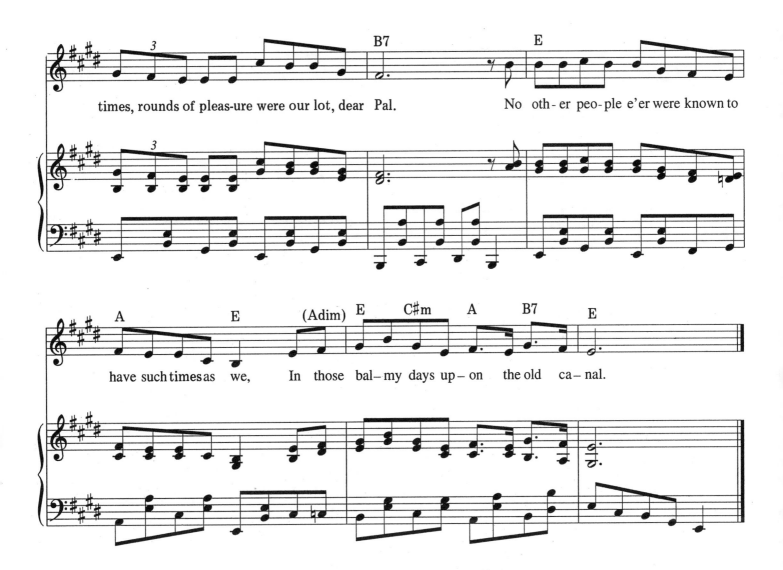

times, rounds of pleas-ure were our lot, dear Pal. No oth-er peo-ple e'er were known to

have such times as we, In those bal—my days up—on the old ca—nal.

My dear friend was forty feet from bank to bank, you know;
Twenty-six at bottom, depth not less than four;
Two feet above the water line, and never more than five,
Towpath ten feet wide, six inches draft, no more.
'Twas always on the lower side of channel, outward pitch,
Clearance fifteen feet, oft twenty more, dear Pal;
Thus making safe our every move from whatever come
We had elbow room along the old canal. *Chorus*

The locks were so majestic, vine-clad, overhanging trees,
Moss and flowers in profusion everywhere;
The song of laughing water rippling and the tumble roar,
Nature smiling, everything without a care.
The birds would join in chorus, katydids and crickets too,
Whippoorwills, owls, frogs their parts would play, dear Pal,
The fish in schools would jump and keep our hooks so bright and nice,
It was great to be upon the old canal. *Chorus*

The locks were fifteen in the clear and ninety foot in length,
Six to twelve foot lift, you'll find this all along.
The boats were the most beautiful, so fairy-like you know.
How they'd blend and serenade in sweetest song!
Our boats, fourteen by eighty feet and eighty tons their load,
But no people had such times as we, dear Pal,
Our fairy palaces were so charming everywhere we went
In those matchless days upon the old canal. *Chorus*

And now whene'er I hear someone reproach or speak unkind
Of this grand old sire, I know they're not informed,
For behold! the towns and cities that are standing on his shores.
Were it not for him they never would be borned.
"He has outlived his usefulness," O this I've heard some say,
They have forgotten, the old man betrayed.
I know there's much that he could do and gladden many hearts
If he only had a half a chance today! *Chorus*

Those famous days were pleasant and in fancy I reflect,
See her boats and packets two thousand and more.
Her shipyards, dry-docks, warehouses and many other things
That were needed, all were standing on her shores.
I know my love for her is true, God grant it ne'er shall change!
For most pleasant is her memory, O Pal.
When I check in, O may I rest in peace for evermore
On the shore of my dear friend, the old canal! *Chorus*